REASON AND EMOTION

REASON
AND EMOTION

by
JOHN MACMURRAY

FABER & FABER LIMITED
3 Queen Square
London

First published in 1935
By Faber and Faber Limited
3 Queen Square London W.C.1
First published in this edition 1962
Reissued 1972
Printed in Great Britain by
Latimer Trend & Co Ltd Whitstable
All rights reserved

ISBN 0 571 09993 9 (Faber Paper Covered Edition)
ISBN 0 571 09992 0 (Hard Bound Edition)

PREFACE TO THE SECOND EDITION

THE LECTURES collected in this volume were written and delivered more than thirty years ago. Underlying them and giving them their unity lay the conviction that the contrast we habitually draw between 'reason' and 'emotion' is a false one, and that the error has practical consequences which have always been serious and may soon prove disastrous. For it leads to the conclusion that our emotional life is irrational, and must remain so. In that case the guidance of life and affairs must lie solely with intellect, which should control action in terms of 'rational' principles, suppressing the emotions where they threaten to infect our behaviour with their dangerous irrationality. The proper contrast, I thought, lies between 'intellect' and 'emotion', while 'reason', as that which makes us human, expresses itself in both. This volume was concerned to clarify the notion of emotional rationality, and to explore some of the modifications in our ways of thinking, especially about science, art and religion, which its recognition involves.

In permitting the publication of a new edition, I

wish to say that I have found no reason to change my mind on any of the major issues involved. It seems to me, rather, that the passage of time has underlined the practical consequences of our reliance upon intellectual prowess for the solution of all human problems. In these thirty years our progress in science and technology, in large-scale planning and organization and in administrative capacity has been immense. Yet the net effect has been to bring us steadily nearer to universal catastrophe. The failure is obviously not an intellectual one. Equally clearly it is the effect of emotional factors, of fear and distrust between nations and classes in particular. But we have no remedy except to increase the intellectual effort and so to make the situation worse.

In republishing this book, then, I believe that in spite of many shortcomings in detail it still points in the main in the right direction. It offers no immediate solution. Indeed, in the field which it cultivates no quick and easy solutions are thinkable. But I may still hope that it can offer, not only some important theoretical considerations, but also some practical suggestions which may prove of ultimate value.

JOHN MACMURRAY

Jordans,
Buckinghamshire,
November 6th, 1961

PREFACE

THE PUBLICATION of my broadcast talks in *Freedom in the Modern World* resulted in a considerable number of invitations from various quarters to clear up difficulties which necessarily arose owing to the compressed form of the original talks. Most of the difficulties centred round the position which I took about the function of the emotions in human life and the restatement of ethical principles to which it committed me. In this volume I have collected for publication a number of lectures referring either directly or indirectly to this problem. Some of these are concerned to restate the position about emotional rationality and others to indicate some of its more important applications.

The first three lectures, which I have grouped under the title of 'Reason in the Emotional Life', form a series in which my general position has been developed at greater length than I had hitherto been able to do. This general statement is followed by two lectures which are concerned with the application of the general principle to educational problems, by two which are specifically concerned with sex and the questions which are related to sex, and by two dealing with the relation of art and religion respectively to science. The remaining four lectures are concerned with religion. Their immediate relation to emotional rationality is not perhaps so clear on the surface, but the religious position I have tried to express is directly connected with the recognition of emotional reason, when it is taken in connexion with the fundamental place that emotion holds in religious experience. The last of these lectures, on the 'Conservation of Personality', I have included because I have continually been asked with reference to certain statements in *Freedom in the Modern World* what attitude I took up on the question of personal immortality.

There is inevitably a certain amount of repetition in a book of this kind. I have made no serious attempt to avoid it, partly because it would have tended to spoil the construction of individual lectures and partly because the repetition of the general principles in different connexions and especially with reference to different applications has considerable value in itself. What seems obscure in one context may often become clear in another.

Some of these lectures have already been published, though only in magazines with a limited and special appeal. Their original publication has been duly acknowledged in footnotes, but I should like to thank those responsible for the original publication for their kindness in permitting me to include these papers in this book. I hope that by being collected and set side by side they will help to interpret one another and will reach a wider public than would otherwise have had the opportunity to consider them.

JOHN MACMURRAY

University College,
London.
June 20th, 1935

CONTENTS

REASON IN THE EMOTIONAL LIFE

I

A<small>NY</small> ENQUIRY must have a motive or it could not be carried on at all, and all motives belong to our emotional life. Moreover, if the enquiry is to be satisfactorily carried through, the emotion which provides the motive for it must be an adequate one. Now, most scientific enquiries are concerned with subjects which are not themselves highly charged with emotional significance for the personal life of the enquirer. But when we come to study the emotional life itself this is no longer true. We are enquiring into the motive forces of our own living, and one of these is the motive that sustains our enquiry. For this reason, the subject to which I have chosen to direct your attention is one in which the success of our enquiry is profoundly bound up with the motives which lead us to undertake it. I must therefore begin with a warning. The only way to approach the subject with any hope of success is to grasp from the beginning its relation to the broad and general issues of our social life as a whole. It may even be dangerous to examine our own emotional life from the wrong motives. In this connexion any motive is wrong if it is egocentric or self-interested. We must remember particularly that the desire to improve our individual lives is just as self-interested as any other form of egocentricity. It is the individual reference to ourselves which vitiates the motives, not the quality or character of our interest in ourselves. Our objective and our motive, therefore, must be wider than the success or failure, the discomfort or happiness of our private lives. This is not a moral exhortation. I am trying quite simply to state the condition which must underlie any attempt to understand or to deal with our emotional development. The desire to save our own lives is a complete barrier to understanding our own lives. It infects the enquiry with a prejudice from the beginning. In this sphere particularly it is true that he that would save his life shall lose it.

Whether we like it or not, we are all enmeshed in that network of relation that binds us together to make up human society. We are parts of one great process—the process of human history. Yet one of the strongest prejudices to which we are all prone is to make exceptions in our own case, and to look upon ourselves as outside it. It is an obvious illusion. No one, not even an Englishman, can 'contract out' of history. We ourselves are events in history. Things do not merely happen to us, they happen through us. We have no existence and no significance merely in ourselves. We have our meaning and our being only 'in God'; and part of what that phrase signifies is 'in the process of the world'. In the bewilderment of these times of change and revolution we are apt to peer out from our different shelters and ask fretfully: 'What is happening to us?' It is an irreligious question. It reveals the kind of people we are. If we had instead the kind of minds that asked naturally 'What is God doing through us in his world?' we might be well on the way to receiving an answer. Behind the former question, shaping its character, lies an emotional unreason. The latter question has its form dictated by emotional rationality.

What is emotional reason? The question, I imagine, seems a strange one, and that itself is highly significant. Our lives belong to a stage in human development in which reason has been dissociated from the emotional life and is contrasted with it. Reason means to us thinking and planning, scheming and calculating. It carries our thoughts to science and philosophy, to the counting-house or the battle-field, but not to music and laughter and love. It does not make us think of religion or loyalty or beauty, but rather of that state of tension which knits our brows when we apply our minds to some knotty problem or devise schemes to cope with a difficult situation. We associate reason with a state of mind which is cold, detached and unemotional. When our emotions are stirred we feel that reason is left behind and we enter another world—more colourful, more full of warmth and delight, but also more dangerous. If we become egocentric, if we forget that we are parts of one small part of the development of human life, we shall be apt to imagine that this has always been so and always must be so; that reason is just thinking; that emotion is just feeling; and that these two aspects of our life are in the eternal nature of things distinct and opposite; very apt to come into conflict and requiring to be kept sternly apart. We shall even be in danger of slipping back into a way of thinking from which we had begun to emerge; of thinking that emotion belongs to the animal nature in us, and reason to the divine; that our emotions are unruly and fleshly, the source of evil and disaster, while reason belongs to the divine essence of the thinking mind which raises us above the level of the brutes into communion with the eternal.

Yet, though this seems to be true, it can hardly be the whole truth about the stage of human development to which we belong. For after all, here we are discussing the question. Somehow or other a doubt has arisen, and we have begun to wonder whether we are right in dissociating the two aspects of our experience. We are asking now: 'Is this attitude right? *Is* reason a matter of intellect and logical thought? Is it really separated from the emotional life that surges beneath it in the depths? Or is there reason in the emotional life itself?' Thought has begun to doubt its own monopoly of reason. As soon as that doubt enters the very basis of our civilization begins to shake, and there arises, first dimly in the depths of us, but soon penetrating more and more clearly into consciousness, the cry for a new heaven and a new earth. The doubt and the question mark the opening of a new phase in human development.

We must keep that large prospect before the eyes of our imagination, when we begin to think about the emotional life. We must not think of it only in relation to our own emotional stresses. All of us, if we are really alive, are disturbed now in our emotions. We are faced by emotional problems that we do not know how to solve. They distract our minds, fill us with misgiving, and sometimes threaten to wreck our lives. That is the kind of experience to which we are all committed. If anyone thinks they are peculiar to the difficulties of his own situation, let him overcome his shyness and talk a little about them to other people. He will discover that he is not a solitary unfortunate. We shall make no headway with these questions unless we begin to see them, and keep on seeing them, not as our private difficulties but as the growing pains of a new world of human experience. Our individual tensions are simply the new thing growing through us into the life of mankind. When we can see them steadily in this universal setting, then and then only will our private difficulties become really significant. We shall recognize them as the travail of a new birth for humanity; as the beginning of a new knowledge of ourselves and of God.

If we are to discover the nature of emotional reason we must first be sure about what we mean by reason in general. It is, in the first place, that which distinguishes us from the world of organic life; which makes us men and women—super-organic. It is the characteristic of personal life. This, however, is only a formal statement. We want to know what are the particular ways in which reason reveals itself in human behaviour. One of the most obvious is the power of speech. Another is the capacity to invent and use tools. Another is the power to organize social life. Behind all these there lies the capacity to make a choice of purposes and to discover and apply the means of realizing our chosen ends. We might go on to draw up a list of such peculiarly personal activities; though it would probably not reveal immediately the root from which they all spring. There are, however, certain persistent cultural expressions of human life which are in a special sense characteristic of our rational nature at its best. These are science, art, and religion. This calls attention to one point at least which is highly significant. Whatever is a characteristic and essential expression of human nature must be an expression of reason. We must recognize, then, that if we wish to discover what reason is we must examine religion and art just as much as science. A conception of reason which is applicable to science but not to religion or art must be a false conception, or at least an inadequate one. Now the obvious difference between science on the one hand and art and religion on the other is that science is intellectual while art and religion are peculiarly bound up with the emotional side of human life. They are not primarily intellectual. This at once forces us to conclude that there must be an emotional expression of reason as well as an intellectual one. Thinking is obviously not the only capacity which is characteristically human and personal.

The definition of reason which seems to me most satisfactory is this. Reason is the capacity to behave consciously in terms of the nature of what is not ourselves. We can express this briefly by saying that reason is the capacity to behave in terms of the nature of the object, that is to say, to behave objectively. Reason is thus our capacity for objectivity.[1] When we

[1] A fuller and more technical discussion of this definition can be found in my book, *Interpreting the Universe*, Chapter VI.

wish to determine why anything behaves as it does, we normally assume that it behaves in terms of its own nature. This means that we need only find out how it is constituted to understand why it responds to a particular stimulus in a particular way. We are apt to make the same assumption when we are considering how human beings behave. When we do this we are met by a special difficulty which is usually discussed as the difficulty about the freedom of the will. The controversy about free will is insoluble, not because the facts referred to are irreconcilable, but because the problem itself is wrongly conceived. We are looking for something in the inner constitution of the human being to explain the peculiar nature of his behaviour. We are still assuming that he must necessarily behave in terms of his own nature, like anything else. It is precisely this assumption that is at fault. Reason is the capacity to behave, not in terms of our own nature, but in terms of our knowledge of the nature of the world outside. Let me give you a simple example. A little boy starts to run across a busy street. His mother sees him from the pavement and sees that he is in imminent danger of running in front of a motor car. Her natural impulse is to call out to him in terror. If she did so she would be acting subjectively in terms of her own natural constitution, responding to a stimulus from the environment. But she does not. She recognizes that to shout to the boy would only increase his danger by distracting his attention, so she suppresses her impulse. Her behaviour is rational, because it is determined not by her subjective impulse but by her recognition of the nature of the situation outside her. She acts in terms of the nature of the object.

It is easy to see that science and all the practical applications of science depend upon reason, in the sense in which we have just defined it. Science rests upon the desire to know things in their objective nature. Behind this lies the desire to be able to use what is in the world through a knowledge of its nature, that is to say, the desire to increase our capacity for acting in terms of the nature of the object. The extent to which we can behave in terms of the nature of the world outside us depends, quite obviously, upon the extent of our knowledge of the world outside. Where objective knowledge fails us we can only act subjectively, on impulse. It is thus the effort to create the conditions of rational activity that gives rise to science.

Now, the main difficulty that faces us in the development of a scientific knowledge of the world lies not in the outside world but in our own emotional life. It is the desire to retain beliefs to which we are emotionally attached for some reason or other. It is the tendency to make the wish father to the thought. Science itself, therefore, is emotionally conditioned.

If we are to be scientific in our thoughts, then, we must be ready to subordinate our wishes and desires to the nature of the world. So long as we want things to be other than they are we cannot see things as they are or act in terms of their real nature. We colour the world with our own illusions. Reason demands that our beliefs should conform to the nature of the world, not to the nature of our hopes and ideals.

In this field, therefore, the discovery of truth must be from the subjective side a process of disillusionment. The strength of our opposition to the development of reason is measured by the strength of our dislike of being disillusioned. We should all admit, if it were put to us directly, that it is good to get rid of illusions, but in practice the process of disillusionment is painful and disheartening. We all confess to the desire to get at the truth, but in practice the desire for truth is the desire to be disillusioned. The real struggle centres in the emotional field, because reason is the impulse to overcome bias and prejudice in our own favour, and to allow our feelings and desires to be fashioned by things outside us, often by things over which we have no control. The effort to achieve this can rarely be pleasant or flattering to our self-esteem. Our natural tendency is to feel and to believe in the way that satisfies our impulses. We all like to feel that we are the central figure in the picture, and that our own fate ought to be different from that of everybody else. We feel that life should make an exception in our favour. The development of reason in us means overcoming all this. Our real nature as persons is to be reasonable and to extend and develop our capacity for reason. It is to acquire greater and greater capacity to act objectively and not in terms of our subjective constitution. That is reason, and it is what distinguishes us from the organic world, and makes us super-organic.

It is precisely the same problem that faces us in the field of morality. Morality, after all, is merely a demand for rational behaviour, and its difficulty is only the difficulty of overcoming our own natural bias in favour of ourselves and those we love, and demanding that life shall show us and them special consideration. Morality demands that we should act 'in the light of eternity', that is, in terms of things as they really are and of people as they really are, and not in terms of our subjective inclinations and private sympathies.

Now we can attack the main issue. All life is activity. Mere thinking is not living. Yet thinking, too, is an activity, even if it is an activity which is only real in its reference to activities which are practical. Now, every activity must have an adequate motive, and all motives are emotional. They belong to our feelings, not to our thoughts. At the most our thoughts may restrict and restrain, or direct and guide, our actions. They can determine their form but not their substance. Even this they can only do by rousing emotions which check or alter the primary motives. Thought is always subsidiary to activity even when we are not directly aware of it. The rationality that appears in thought is itself the reflection of a rationality that belongs to the motives of action. It follows that none of our activities, not even the activities of thinking, can express our reason unless the emotions which produce and sustain them are rational emotions.

What can it mean, then, to distinguish between rational and irrational feelings? We are in the habit of saying that our feelings are just felt. They can't be either true or false; they just are what they are. Our thoughts, on the other hand, can be true or false. About that we have no difficulty. Yet, if we think carefully, we shall realize that there is no special difference between feelings and thoughts in this respect. Our thoughts are just what we think. We just think them, and they are what they are. How then can they be either true or false? The answer is that their truth or falsity does not lie in them but in a relation between them and the things to which they refer. True thoughts are thoughts which refer properly to reality, and which are thought in terms of the nature of the object to which they refer. Why should our feelings be in any different case? It is true that they are felt and that they are what they are felt to be, just like our thoughts. But they also refer to things outside us. If I am angry I am angry at something or somebody, though I may not always be able to say precisely what it is. Thought is similar. We are often unable to say precisely what it is that we are thinking about, but it is always something. Since our feelings, then, refer to what is outside them, to some object about which they are felt, why should they not refer rightly or wrongly to their object, just like thoughts? Why should they not be proper feelings when they are in terms of the nature of the object, and improper feelings when they are not in terms of the nature of the object? When we put it in this way, we recognize that this is a distinction which we are always making. To a person who is terribly afraid of a mouse we are quite accustomed to say that there is nothing really to be afraid of. Her fear is not in terms of the real nature of the situation. It is subjective. We can acknowledge, therefore, without any difficulty, that feelings can be rational or irrational in precisely the same way as thoughts, through the correctness or incorrectness of their reference to reality. In thinking thoughts we think the things to which the thoughts refer. In feeling emotions we feel the things to which the emotions refer. And, therefore, we can feel rightly or wrongly. The only one of the great philosophers who recognized this parallelism between thought and feeling, and who maintained that our feelings could be true or false, was Plato. He insisted on it both in the *Republic* and in the *Philebus*. This view of Plato's has usually been treated by commentators as a forgivable eccentricity in Plato's thought, like his attitude to art and artists. It seems to me not merely true but of much more profound significance than Plato himself recognized. It is not that our feelings have a secondary and subordinate capacity for being rational or irrational. It is that reason is primarily an affair of emotion, and that the rationality of thought is the derivative and secondary one. For if reason is the capacity to *act* in terms of the nature of the object, it is emotion which stands directly behind activity determining its substance and direction, while thought is related to action indirectly and through emotion, determining only its form, and that only partially.

The chief difficulty in the development of emotional reason lies in the surprising fact that we know relatively little about our own emotional life. We are apt to know more about other people's. It is a commonplace that in all matters which touch us closely it is very difficult to be sure of our own motives. Rather than admit to motives which would injure our self-esteem we prevent them from entering our consciousness or allow them to appear only in forms which disguise and misrepresent their real nature. Modern psychology has been very much concerned to develop various technical methods of overcoming the forces which repress these motives, and its success has been sufficient at least to reveal to what an extent our emotional life is unconscious. But in fact psychoanalysis has only extended and developed a knowledge which we all possess. We continually recognize in other people motives and feelings of which they themselves are quite ignorant. Let me illustrate this by a story of my own invention. It is about three friends, Jane and Josephine and Peter. They are all young. Jane is wealthy and influential. Josephine is a struggling young artist. Both of them are interested in Peter, and Peter is interested in both of them. Josephine has long cherished a desire to continue her art studies in Rome and has applied for a scholarship which would enable her to go. But she is torn between her desire to go abroad and her growing interest in Peter. Jane uses her influence to get the scholarship for Josephine, and succeeds. She carries the good news to Josephine and in great excitement tells her how hard she had worked to get it for her. She is very astonished and hurt to find that Josephine receives the news very coldly and is not properly grateful. At that Jane feels very angry with Josephine.

Jane confides all this to a friend of hers called Peggy. Peggy suggests that the explanation is a simple one. Josephine is feeling sad at having to leave her friends and has been growing very fond of Peter.

Jane admits that Josephine is fond of Peter but feels quite sure that that can't be the reason. Josephine, she says, would never allow anything of that kind to interfere with her art. In any case, it is very good for Peter that she should go. Peter is very sensitive and Josephine's artistic temperament plays havoc with his nerves. Jane has often noticed it. Indeed when she was working to get the scholarship for Josephine, she had Peter's welfare in her mind too. Whether Josephine is grateful or not, she doesn't care. She is proud to have been able to serve both her friends.

What was Jane's real motive? All her friends told themselves—and each other—what it was. But did Jane know? Probably not at all. She would have been very hurt if anyone had presumed to enlighten her. At any rate there is no need for me to explain. The point of the story for our present purpose is this: the reasons we give ourselves for our activities, and even more certainly the reasons we give to other people for them, rarely express our real motive, and never the whole of our motive. When we ask ourselves why we behaved as we did, we often find ourselves insisting to ourselves, with a certain inner stress, upon the reasons that we give. That feeling of insistence is always adequate evidence that the real motive is a different one, and one that is hidden from ourselves. Such hidden motives are necessarily subjective. They are necessarily the expression not of reason but of subjective impulses. They cannot be in terms of our conscious recognition of the true nature of the situation.

It is extremely difficult to become aware of this great hinterland of our minds, and to bring our emotional life, and with it the motives which govern our behaviour, fully into consciousness. This is peculiarly true of contemporary people. It is not nearly so true of primitive men. The nineteenth century in particular was the climax of a long period of social repression in which the intellectual development of reason was the main effort and the emotional life was considered chiefly as an intrusive force which prevented the achievement of that calmness which is necessary for the proper functioning of thought. But that development itself brings us back at last to the emotional life. The development of science finally must direct its attention to personality itself; and as soon as it does this it is directed upon the emotional sources of all personal activity. It is because it is so difficult for us to bring our unconscious motives into consciousness that at last we find ourselves driven to make the attempt. That is why so much of the interest of contemporary life is centred upon emotional experience. It means the beginning of the task of developing emotional reason in man. In this, as in most things, it is the first step that is the most difficult. Jane's emotional development will begin when she realizes that she was jealous of Josephine and wanted to get her out of the way. The probable effect of this realization will be that she will say to herself 'What a horrible little worm I am', and begin to revel in despising herself. Such self-abasement is just as unreasonable, perhaps even more unreasonable, than her previous state of mind. It is a compensation which still enables her to be concerned with herself. It is still childish, immature and egocentric. Self-pity and self-disgust are just as irrational as self-assertion. The real problem of the development of emotional reason is to shift the centre of feeling from the self to the world outside. We can only begin to grow up into rationality when we begin to see our own emotional life not as the centre of things but as part of the development of humanity.

The field in which emotional reason expresses itself most directly is the field of art. The artist is directly concerned to express his emotional experience of the world. His success depends upon the rationality of his emotions. It is not enough that the artist should express his emotional reaction to the world. If his feelings are merely subjective reactions, his work will be bad. What will make it valuable or significant is the way in which his emotions refer to the world. The artist expresses the nature of the objective world as apprehended in emotion. As a result, our own experience of works of art shows the same distinction between those which affect us subjectively and those which reveal the world to us in its real significance. Some pictures, for instance, we appreciate because they touch off in our minds associations which are pleasant and exciting. They act upon us merely as a stimulus to thoughts and feelings which we enjoy for their own sake. But such pictures are artistically bad. There are others which move us in an entirely different way, because they contain their significance in themselves. They do not set us to enjoy our own feelings. They make us enjoy *themselves*, and they refer us to the significance of the world outside.

These true works of art are more difficult to appreciate. They do something to us, often, if they are contemporary; something that we object to. They involve some disillusionment that we dislike, and they are not immediately exciting. They deny us the opportunity of revelling in our own sensations and force us to be objective. The reason is that objective emotion is not a mere reaction to a stimulus. It is an immediate appreciation of the value and significance of real things. Emotional reason is our capacity to apprehend objective values. This point, important as it is, I have no time to develop at length. I must conclude by drawing your attention to its final expression in our relations with one another. Love, which is the fundamental positive emotion characteristic of human beings, can be either subjective and irrational, or objective and rational. In feeling love for another person, I can either experience a pleasurable emotion which he stimulates in me, or I can love *him*. We have, therefore, to ask ourselves, is it really the other person that I love, or is it myself? Do I enjoy him or do I enjoy myself in being with him? Is he just an instrument for keeping me pleased with myself, or do I feel his existence and his reality to be important in themselves? The difference between these two kinds of love is the ultimate difference between organic and personal life. It is the difference between rational and irrational emotion. The capacity to love objectively is the capacity which makes us persons. It is the ultimate source of our capacity to behave in terms of the object. It is the core of rationality.

REASON IN THE EMOTIONAL LIFE

II

I HAVE TRIED to show you that the capacity for reason belongs to our emotional nature, just as much as to the intellect. Our feelings may be illusory, just as our intellectual ideas often are. Our emotions can be real or unreal. To say that a feeling is unreal does not mean that we do not feel it, any more than to say that an idea is false means that we do not think it. An unreal or illusory emotion may be very strongly felt, and it may influence our conduct profoundly. It is the feelings that we do feel and which do provide the motives of our activities that are often unreal. You know what it is like to come downstairs in the dark and think you are on the last step when you are actually on the last but one. You step on to empty air where you thought there was solid ground. Something like that often happens to us in the emotional field. We find suddenly in action that our feelings do not correspond to the real situation at all.

Now if that is so, the question arises: 'How can we

see to it that our emotions are not illusory? How can we train ourselves to have feelings which do correspond to the nature of the situation in which we act? How can we develop an emotional life that is reasonable in itself, so that it moves us to forms of behaviour which are appropriate to reality? Or, to put the same point from a different angle, how can we be trained in our emotional life to recognize the real values in the world around us?'

The first condition of any attempt to answer these questions is that we should really recognize that our emotional life does need educating; that our feelings, emotions and passions are often nonsensical; that they do not correspond to anything real. We must really believe that a great many of our feelings ought not to be felt, and that our ordinary apprehension of values is very poor and often false. We must admit, at least, that our feelings are always liable to be wrong. We feel that something is beautiful when it is not, and ugly when it is not. We are liable to be shocked by things that are not really shocking, or to be terrified when there is really nothing to be afraid of. On the other hand, we are often emotionally blind. We fail, very often, to feel anything at all when we ought to be profoundly moved. We notice this when somebody points it out to us. Besides this, we are full of vague and indefinite feelings which we fail to recognize for what they are, and as a result we often think we are feeling one thing when we are really feeling something else. We misrepresent our real feelings to ourselves. We have then to distinguish three different ways in which our emotional life may be unreal. We may have clear and definite feelings which are illusory. We may have feelings which we misrepresent and mistake; and we may be too insensitive to have feelings that are called for by the nature of the situation. I must therefore repeat what I said in my first lecture, that we are very apt to take the view that one feels what one feels, and that's all there is about it. If one is jealous, for instance, one is just jealous, and it can't be helped. One must just make the best one can of the situation. Now that isn't so. There is in the emotional life itself a capacity for growth and development. What is apt to blind us to this is simply that it is impossible to be in error and to know that we are in error at the same time. That is true in the intellectual field. We cannot believe something that we know to be false. It is equally true in the emotional field. If, for example, we feel very angry or ashamed, and our anger or shame is an unreal emotion, then we cannot know that it is unreal. If something shocks us which is in fact not shocking, it is precisely because we do feel shocked that our feeling is false. There is no way of revealing the falseness of our emotions except in the process of changing them.

In the second place, we must notice that we cannot

35

fall back upon thinking in this dilemma. I do not mean that thought can do nothing. It can, indeed, help us to get a clear view of the nature of the thing that is responsible for our emotion, and very often our feelings go wrong because we mistake one thing for another, or because we do not know the true facts. But thinking can never do more than improve our knowledge of the facts of the situation, and even this is difficult where our emotions are strongly aroused, because the emotion itself tends to make thinking difficult, or to pervert it if the emotion is unreasonable. Under these circumstances we tend to insist that the situation is what we feel it is, often against the clearest intellectual evidence that we are wrong. But apart from the difficulty of using thought in the field where it might help us, there is one crucial thing that thinking cannot do at all. It cannot decide whether the thing it reveals is good or bad, beautiful or ugly, to be shunned or to be sought. For the determination of values we are dependent on our emotions—or on those of someone else. It often seems as though we use our intellectual judgment to decide that something is good or bad, even when our emotions disagree with our judgment. But in that case what we are doing is to apply a standard of judgment which is itself derived from other emotions, perhaps our own earlier ones, perhaps those of other people, and very often the emotions of people long since dead which have become traditionally standardized. A judgment of value can never be intellectual in its origin, though of course the intellect can formulate as standards of judgment the types of action which have in the past been recognized emotionally as good or bad. Our judgments of value are necessarily emotional, though the emotions that they express are not necessarily those that we happen to be feeling at the moment. They may easily be other people's, and express emotions which we ourselves have never felt at all. How many people would maintain stoutly that Milton's *Paradise Lost* is a very beautiful poem, who have never read it, or have been bored by it when they did! From this we may at least draw one important conclusion. There can be no hope of educating our emotions unless we are prepared to stop relying on other people's for our judgments of value. We must learn to feel for ourselves even if we make mistakes.

How, then, are we to educate and develop our emotional life so that we can trust our feelings to reveal the values of the world to us? To answer that question I must begin by drawing attention to an aspect of our experience which is too much overlooked and yet in which the root of the whole matter lies. I refer to the use we make of our senses and of our sense-experience. The education of our emotional life is primarily an education of our sensibility. It is the training of our sensuality. I use the word sensuality deliberately, because the recoil that it is apt to produce in our feelings helps to reveal the difficulty. Sensuality means properly the capacity to enjoy organic experience, to enjoy the satisfaction of the senses. But there lies behind us a long tradition which would persuade us that this capacity is undesirable, and should be eliminated altogether. It will have it that we ought to get rid of the desire to satisfy our senses, that we should be trained to suppress our sensuality, and to prevent it from issuing in action. As a result of that tradition, the word has come to have a shameful meaning, and has acquired the power to shock us when we hear it used. It has come to be associated in our minds with the lack of self-control and with an immoderate and vulgar indulgence in bodily pleasures. We had better, therefore, put it aside as one of those words which has been ruined by misuse and employ instead the term sensibility, even though that word also has its disadvantages. The trouble with the word sensibility is that it suggests something much too 'refined'. I used the word sensuality to draw attention to the way in which it had degenerated in its application, and to point out that this degeneration is itself strong evidence of a persistent attitude to the organic and sensuous aspect of our experience which makes the development of the emotional life impossible. For it implies that the satisfaction of the senses is somehow bad in itself and, therefore, incapable of being developed into anything of value. It suggests that the impulse to sensuous satisfaction should be hidden away and kept under lock and key. The first stage in any education of the emotional life must be the reversal of this attitude. We have to start by recognizing and insisting that the life of the senses is inherently good, and that instead of keeping our sensibility under an iron control, we should allow it to develop in its own freedom. I do not suggest that the normal sensibility of adult Europeans at the present time is anything to be proud of. What I do believe is that it is under-developed and irrational because of the way we have treated it. Only a faculty that is free to exercise itself can be educated.

The senses are the gateways of our awareness. They are the avenues along which we move into contact with the world around us. Without this sensuous awareness of the world, no consciousness and no knowledge of any kind is possible, for human beings at least. Even our knowledge of God is only possible through the awareness of the world which our senses provide. We see and hear, taste and smell and touch the world. This is the foundation of our conscious life. If we did not do this thing there would be no world at all, as far as we are concerned, and neither would there be us. This is of course a truism. But like so many truisms it is left behind and forgotten when we begin to think. I want to emphasize its importance. Our sense-life is central and fundamental to our human experience. The richness and fullness of our lives depends especially upon the richness and fullness, upon the delicacy and quality of our sense-life. If we see and hear thinly or crudely or narrowly, our own nature will be thin and crude and narrow, however hard we work the inner processes. The senses provide the material out of which the inner life is built. It is of no use to instal the latest machinery in the mill if the corn you have to grind is poor, blighted and unhealthy. It is no use to have a highly trained mind if the material it works upon is poor in quality and meagre in amount. 'I am come', said Jesus, 'that they might have life, and that they might have it more abundantly.' The abundance of our life depends primarily upon the abundance of our sensuous experience of the world around us. If we are to be full of life and fully alive, it is the increase in our capacity to be aware of the world through our senses which has first to be achieved.

Now, there are two distinct ways in which we can employ our senses; a thin and narrow way, and a full and complete way. The thin way comes from restricting the senses to the use we can make of them for practical purposes. We have a marvellous capacity for failing to notice what stares us in the face, if it is not immediately related to the purpose and interest that dominates our minds. If the interest is narrowly practical, what we perceive in the world will be a narrow range of utilizable facts. The fuller and wider way of using our senses is to live in them for the sake of the experience, to use them for the joy of using them. In the first case our senses are specialized instruments for achieving definite, prescribed purposes. We use our eyes to look for something we have lost, to gain information about how we can cross a busy street, and so on. We use our ears to gain information that will be useful to us in furthering our ends, and become deaf to everything else. Sense-awareness, in that case, is only a means to an end. Its value for us lies not in the awareness itself but in the things it enables us to do. We may call this the practical or scientific use of the senses, in which they provide, on the theoretical side, data which can be elaborated by thought into a general theory; and on the practical side, facts which we must take into account in planning for action and in acting.

But when we use our senses just to become aware of what is around us, for the sake of the awareness itself, we use them in a different and fuller way. We can look at things for the joy of seeing them; we can listen to the sounds of the world because it is good to hear them, without any ulterior motive or special purpose. In that case, we look at things not

because we want to use them but because we want to
see them. We touch things because we want to feel
them. Sensitive awareness becomes then a life in
itself with an intrinsic value of its own which we
maintain and develop for its own sake, because it is a
way of living, perhaps the very essence of all living.
When we use our senses in this way we come alive
in them, as it were, and this opens up a whole new
world of possibility. We see and hear and feel things
that we never noticed before, and find ourselves taking
delight in their existence. We find ourselves living
in our senses for love's sake, because the essence of
love lies in this. When you love anyone you want
above all things to be aware of him, more and more
completely and delicately. You want to see him and
hear him, not because you want to make use of him
but simply because that is the natural and only way
of taking delight in his existence for his sake. That is
the way of love, and it is the only way of being alive.
Life, when it is really lived, consists in this glad
awareness. Living through the senses is living in love.
When you love anything, you want to fill your consciousness with it. You want to affirm its existence.
You feel that it is good that it should be in the world
and be what it is. You want other people to look at it
and enjoy it too. You want to look at it again and
again. You want to know it, to know it better and
better, and you want other people to do the same.

In fact, you are appreciating and enjoying it for *itself*, and that is all that you want. This kind of knowledge is primarily of the senses. It is not of the intellect. You don't want merely to know about the object; often you don't want to know about it at all. What you do want is to know *it*. Intellectual knowledge tells us about the world. It gives us knowledge *about* things, not knowledge *of* them. It does not reveal the world as it is. Only emotional knowledge can do that. The use of the senses as a practical means of getting knowledge is thus not a way of knowing the world at all, but only a way of knowing about it. The wider use of the senses for the joy of living in them, is knowing the world itself in and through emotion, not by means of the intellect. This is not to disparage intellectual knowledge but only to insist that it is meaningless and without significance, apart from the direct sensual knowledge which gives it reality. One cannot really know about anything unless one first knows it. Intellectual awareness is egocentric. It uses the senses as its instrument. But the direct sensual awareness has its centre in the world outside, in the thing that is sensed and loved for its own sake. There is a drawing of George Morrow's which illustrates the difference humorously. It shows a couple standing on a hilltop watching a sunset. The sky is aglow with bars of bright clouds. 'What a lovely sunset,' the woman says to her husband. 'That reminds me,' he answers. 'Do remember to tell our landlady that I like my bacon streaky.'

The fundamental element in the development of the emotional life is the training of this capacity to live in the senses, to become more and more delicately and completely aware of the world around us, because it is a good half of the meaning of life to be so. It is a training in sensitiveness; which is a very different thing from accurate observation. The reason is that awareness is directly related to action and that our modes of awareness determine our modes of action. If we limit awareness so that it merely feeds the intellect with the material for thought, our actions will be intellectually determined. They will be mechanical, planned, thought-out. Our sensitiveness is being limited to a part of ourselves—the brain in particular—and, therefore, we will act only with part of ourselves, at least so far as our actions are consciously and rationally determined. If, on the other hand, we live in awareness, seeking the full development of our sensibility to the world, we shall soak ourselves in the life of the world around us; with the result that we shall act with the whole of ourselves. The author of a recent book,[1] in explaining how she discovered this in her own experience, says that she found herself listening to music through the soles of

[1] *A Life of One's Own*, by Joanna Field.

her feet. If you have any inkling of what that means you will understand me when I say that we have to learn to live with the whole of our bodies, not only with our heads. If we do this, we shall find ourselves able to act in the world with the whole of our bodies, and our actions will be spontaneous, emotional, non-mechanical and free. Intellectually controlled action, in fact, is only possible through the process of inhibition. The intellect itself cannot be a source of action. All motives of action are necessarily emotional, but the intellect can use the emotion of fear to paralyse the positive emotions, leaving only that one free to determine action which corresponds to the planned purpose. Such action can never be creative, because creativeness is a characteristic which belongs to personality in its wholeness, acting as a whole, and not to any of its parts acting separately.

Now, all *real* action is creative, and it is only possible in relation to direct sensuous awareness. You will see this principle at work very simply in the way that children (and grown-ups too, whenever they are surprised out of their frustration and preoccupations) dance and sing. Their wholeness and their direct awareness of the world expresses itself in action which is graceful and beautiful, because they are emotionally alive and in direct contact with the world. There is nothing strange or marvellous about this. That is the way human beings are made. If they don't

45

behave in that natural way something has gone wrong, something has produced a partial stoppage of the awareness of reality in them. If we allow ourselves to be completely sensitive and completely absorbed in our awareness of the world around, we have a direct emotional experience of the real value in the world, and we respond to this by behaving in ways which carry the stamp of reason upon them in their appropriateness and grace and freedom. The creative energy of the world absorbs us into itself and acts through us. This, I suppose, is what people mean by 'inspiration'. If it is, it is the most natural thing in life.

The education of the emotions, then, consists in the cultivation of a direct sensitiveness to the reality of the world around us. The reason why our emotional life is so undeveloped, is that we habitually suppress a great deal of our sensitiveness and train our children from their earliest years to suppress much of their own. It might seem strange that we should cripple ourselves so heavily in this way. But there is a simple reason for it which I want to mention in closing. We are afraid of what would be revealed to us if we did not. In imagination we feel sure that it would be lovely to live with a full and rich awareness of the world. But in practice sensitiveness hurts. It is not possible to develop the capacity to see beauty without developing also the capacity to see ugliness, for they are the same capacity. The capacity for joy is also the capacity for pain. We soon find that any increase in our sensitiveness to what is lovely in the world increases also our capacity for being hurt. That is the dilemma in which life has placed us. We must choose between a life that is thin and narrow, uncreative and mechanical, with the assurance that even if it is not very exciting it will not be intolerably painful; and a life in which the increase in its fullness and creativeness brings a vast increase in delight, but also in pain and hurt. People have always sought for some way of life in which pleasure could be increased and pain avoided, and the whole philosophy of Utilitarianism is an elaborate effort to persuade us that it is possible. The maximum of pleasure with the minimum of pain for the greatest possible number of people is the ideal of the Utilitarian. The Nemesis that waits upon it is this, that we must choose between the increase of pleasure and the avoidance of pain. If we choose to minimize pain we must damp down human sensitiveness, and so limit the sources of possible delight. If we decide to increase our joy in life we can only do it by accepting a heightened sensitiveness to pain. On the whole we seem to have chosen to seek the absence of pain, and as a result we have produced stagnation and crudity.

REASON IN THE EMOTIONAL LIFE

III

I N THIS lecture I propose to deal with the two great cultural aspects of life which both foreshadow and depend upon our capacity for emotional reason—art and religion. What I have said already can be summarized briefly. Reason—the capacity in us which makes us human—is not in any special sense a capacity of the intellect. It is not our power of thinking, though it expresses itself in our thinking as well as in other ways. It must also express itself in our emotional life, if that is to be human. Emotion is not the Cinderella of our inner life, to be kept in her place among the cinders in the kitchen. Our emotional life is *us* in a way our intellectual life cannot be; in that it alone contains the motives from which our conduct springs. Reason reveals itself in emotion by its objectivity, by the way it corresponds to and apprehends reality. Reason in the emotional life determines our behaviour in terms of the real values of the world in which we live. It discovers and reveals goodness and badness, right and wrong, beauty and ugliness and all the infinite variety of values of which these are only the rough, general, intellectual abstractions. The development of *human* nature in its concrete livingness is, in fact, the development of emotional reason.

I have also pointed out that our organic, sensual consciousness is the special means through which both our intellectual and our emotional life makes contact with the real world outside us. When we use our sensibility as a means to achieving purposes we cut off our emotional life from direct contact with the world outside, and so from the possibility of developing its own inherent reason. We must, of course, do this often to achieve specific ends. But if we allow this mediate awareness to dictate the general form of our living, then we frustrate our emotional development. We prevent the growth in us of the capacity to recognize and distinguish good and bad. We become blind to value. Reason develops in the emotional life by living in the sensibility, by the exercise of our sensitiveness to the world; and that means by living in the world with our whole sensuous capacity.

That mode of exercising our sensuous capacity in which we are being conscious for the sake of being conscious; in which no justification in terms of a purpose is needed because it is life in itself, which is beyond justification—that mode of awareness for its own sake is directly connected with our emotional life, and it provides at once the relation between our emotions and the reality of the world which calls the reason in them into play. I suggested, too, that this emotional reason expresses itself, under these conditions, in activity which is itself rational; and that the hall-mark of such reasonful action is its beauty or gracefulness—in fact, its 'appropriateness'. Such actions are, again, not means to an end, but ways of being alive in action. Thus the training of the emotions is primarily a training in the capacity of sensitiveness to the object. For by living in our senses I do not mean using our senses for the pleasure they can give us. That is the opposite of what I mean; precisely what we want to get away from. That is only another way of using the senses for an ulterior motive—the motive of self-gratification. I mean, rather, maintaining and increasing our sensitiveness to the world outside, irrespective of whether it gives us pleasure or pain. I mean keeping as fully alive to things as they are, whether they are pleasant or unpleasant, as we possibly can. I mean being open to *reality*.

Now, art and religion are the two aspects of human reason in which such awareness is sought and expressed. It will throw considerable light, therefore, on the nature of emotional reason if we can understand art and religion in relation to the activities of human nature out of which they spring. Unfortunately the very first thing that confronts us in this is the fact that our way of regarding art and religion bears witness to the absence of emotional reason. One of the clearest characteristics of subjective attitudes is that they are egocentric. We are egocentric when we regard the world as existing for our private satisfaction; as a means to our individual ends. The development of reason consists precisely in the process of overcoming this self-centredness and becoming able increasingly to escape from our natural bias in our own favour. So long as we think that art and religion are concerned with our pleasure or our consolation; so long as we look on them as activities of our own or of other people which give us something that we want; which make *us* happy, or protect, or comfort us, we are in a subjective and irrational frame of mind. Now this is the way that most of us do regard art and religion (and science too, for that matter). We look upon art as a decoration and a beautifying of our lives. Beautiful things are made for our delight. That is how we look at the matter. Our treatises on Beauty start off, almost without exception, by assuming that the real question about art is why it gives us pleasure; and proceed to try to distinguish good art from bad by the kind of pleasurable effect it has on the spectator or the listener.

That is an egocentric attitude. Similarly in religion. Most of us think of religion as giving us something; as consoling us in trouble; helping us in difficulties, strengthening us in the face of death, and so on. As if God existed for our sakes! As if our success and our safety and our happiness were the meaning of the whole world! So long as we look to art and religion in this way—for the satisfaction of our private desires, our *natural* private desires—we can't begin to understand what they are, and all our ideas about them will be delusions, expressing only our vanity and self-conceit.

Art and religion are ways of living the personal life—and I mean by that the life of rational consciousness, the real life of human beings. The question is not 'What use is art or religion to us?' but 'What is it in us that demands and produces art and religion?' What is it in our nature that insists that we should seek after beauty and after God? My first answer to this question is that it is simply the natural impulse to fulfil our own being, to be rational creatures, to achieve personality. Primarily it is a blind urge towards reason; and it is the force in us that makes us human beings at all. It is that drive in us that makes us seek reality and be dissatisfied with illusions and unrealities in ourselves and in the world. We are made to be reasonable creatures—to live a life of objective consciousness. Because of this there is in us a need to be aware of the world—and to live in that awareness and by it.

Now, art and religion are two aspects of this search for the life of rational personality. They are the efforts of our sensitiveness to live in the knowledge of the reality of which we are part. They are efforts to express the life of reason in us. They are alike in this, that they seek the awareness of reality through our emotional sensitiveness. They are the expressions of reason working in the emotional life in search of reality. Because we are persons it is not enough to have a feeling. We are driven to ask: 'What is it in the world that this feeling is about?' It is not enough to feel fear like an animal and then turn tail and run. We have to ask: 'What am I afraid of, and is it really to be feared?' The reason working in our emotional life forces us to take our feelings as an awareness of things outside us, as a consciousness of the meaning and value of things other than ourselves. So, on the basis of our emotional consciousness of the world we become artists and we become worshippers of God. Art and religion arise as ways of behaving as rational beings, as ways of expressing in our modes of living our awareness of the significance of the world we live in, an awareness which we possess through the reason in our emotional life. They are ways of expressing our emotional rationality.

But we must not suppose that the expressions we

have found, or that men have found in the past are true and adequate expressions. That would be very unlikely. It would be just as absurd to suppose that the ideas men have had about the nature of the world or the ideas they have now, were true and adequate ideas. The ancient Indians thought that the world rested on an elephant, and the elephant on a tortoise. That belief was the expression of the reason in them seeking an explanation of the world. It is grounded in the impulse to reason that creates science. Yet it is a childish explanation of a crude kind. We must remember that it is not merely truth but also error that we owe to reason. Only a rational being can be subject to error, illusion or mistake. And this is equally true in the emotional field. The expressions of the working of reason in our emotional life are likely to be childish and crude and grotesque at first. That only means that they are immature. After all, science only came into being as a mature expression of the intellectual search for reality a few centuries ago. And it was born through the discovery of what the intellect is after and how we must set to work— systematically and methodically—if the rational demand for objective knowledge of fact is to be achieved. It was only then that intellectual reason ceased to be a series of shots in the dark by unusually gifted men, each saying his say and being contra- dicted by the others. And it is characteristic of that coming of age of intellectual reason that it resulted from a recognition of ignorance, and substituted the humility that knows that its best theories are only more or less probable, for the dogmatism that thought it had the truth, the whole truth and nothing but the truth.

I believe, therefore, that in art and religion mankind is still in the stage of immaturity. There has been no true art and no true religion established yet in the world. And one of the strongest reasons that I have for saying so is precisely that we are so sure that we are right in these fields. We are so confident that we know what is right and what is wrong; and yet we all contradict one another over it. We are so sure that our notions about God and about what pleases and displeases him are *the* truth. It is worth while to remember that one of the signs of a subjective consciousness is its habit of swinging from the heights of confidence to the depths of despair. So we are either entirely confident that our religion is absolutely true, or afraid that it may be a complete illusion. We swing from a childish credulity to an equally childish agnosticism. That is a proof of the failure to be rational in our emotional awareness. Religion and art, in their mature forms, are still in the future. What we have yet is only the groping of reason in the dark after reality. And when art and religion reach their maturity, the sign by which we shall know them is our discovery of our ignorance, the falling away of our dogmatism and the realization of the meaning of our search. Men will begin to know what they are after in art and religion; to know that they haven't got it; but also to know that by humble, patient, methodical search together they may gradually reach towards a common awareness of the reality of beauty and of God. Still, in art and in religion our way to reality lies through disillusionment. We have yet to discover that our sense of values, our feelings for good and evil, for right and wrong, for beauty and ugliness, are largely illusory, or, if they are true, it is by accident, because we do not really *know* whether they are true or false. We are, I think, near that recognition in the field of art. We are yet far from it in the religious field. For us, therefore, the search for beauty and for God must remain first and foremost a search, in which the main result is likely to be the discovery of the falsehood of our certainties, and through that the discovery of what we are really searching for without finding it. It is something unknown—something new and undiscovered—that we are after. And so far as we get glimpses of it we will have to create new forms of expression. The old ones are useless. Men do not put new wine in old bottles.

I cannot, of course, go on to reveal the thing which man has to discover, either in art or in religion. I am in no privileged position. We are all in the stage of

discovering our own blindness. We live as best we
may, by the traditional habits of English life. Our
feelings work in the main in the established subjective mode; even when intellectually we know that
we cannot trust them. We all have occasional moments when in a flash we see the new thing, as if in a
mirage, and wonder whether it is only a trick of the
imagination. And all I can say about these moments
of vision is that they suggest a new heaven and a
new earth. They do not reveal anything very
definite. But they do show up the kind of human life
we do lead and the values by which we work, as
devastatingly mean and poverty-stricken and ridiculous; so that afterwards we remain haunted by a conviction that whatever the reality of human life may
be, the kind of life we live in Europe in the twentieth
century is a fantastic travesty of it. In our ways of
living we have certainly not grasped the significance
of life. We are leagues away from any knowledge of
the good; and of what beauty is we have only fantastic illusions. We cannot escape from the negative
character of the life we all live together. Nor do we
know how to live otherwise.

But I can perhaps help towards an intellectual
understanding of art and religion; towards the discovery of what they would be if we could achieve
them by the growth to maturity of our emotional
reason. Art, it seems to me, is always a search for the

value in the individual things with which the world
is stored. I am not speaking now of works of art but
of the thing that is happening in the artist. He is
emotionally contemplative. He fills his senses with an
object or a set of objects, and seeks to feel it; to become emotionally aware of its being, and to realize
it fully as that individual thing. That is his attitude
to the world, when he is being an artist. He wants to
go out to it, to soak himself in it and so to become
emotionally conscious of its meaning and significance
in itself. He is not trying to discover things about it
but to know it as something that exists in its own
right, something that is part of the furniture of earth
and therefore has its value in itself—not for him or
for anyone else. His success depends entirely upon his
ability to get outside himself, as it were—to lose himself in what he sees, and to feel its nature and its life.
So far as he can do this he finds that it has the result
of producing in him a spontaneous creative activity
which expresses the awareness of the thing which he
has achieved. If he paints a picture, what the picture
says is not 'This is what the object looks like; so, if you
have seen this you needn't look at the object'; it says
rather: 'I have known something—really known it—
and this is what it means in itself. Look at this and
you will realize the significance of the thing as it
revealed itself to me.' And this suggests at once what
the development of art signifies in human life. It

represents the effort to become aware of the significance of individuals in themselves through an emotional apprehension of them. Art expresses to us our capacity as rational beings to apprehend the values of things in themselves; not their value to us but their meaning and significance in their own right as individuals in the world. It expresses that rational impulse in us to delight in the things that are real individuals in the world just because they are there and reveal themselves to us. A mature art, if we achieve it, as we have now achieved a mature science, would be our way of reaching nearer and nearer, through the co-operative effort of many individuals, to a real emotional knowledge of the significance of real things.

What then of religion? Religion, I think, is all this and something more. We can understand it best if we start from the limitation of art. Art is essentially individual and contemplative. The artistic attitude is that of the looker-on, admiring and loving what it sees, but not participating in the life that it contemplates, except in imagination, subjectively. And as a result art has to go from one individual to another and realize each for itself and in itself; but not in its togetherness with other things to make up a whole world. The artist also cannot co-operate in his activity. He is solitary in it, of necessity. Suppose then that the object that the artistic consciousness is seeking to feel and apprehend for itself is another human being. Don't think of art in the ordinary sense. Think rather of yourself lovingly watching other people in the artist's way—admiring them, trying to feel what they are in themselves; not wanting them for yourself; seeking to appreciate them. Under what conditions is this possible? Simply that they should be unaware of you; that they should be living their own lives, carrying on their own activity as if you weren't there, watching. The moment they notice that you are watching them something enters that alters the whole situation. You are now two people aware of one another: the emotional awareness is mutual, and with it comes self-consciousness. The watcher is being watched by his object. The consciousness is not one-sided; it is a consciousness *between* two people—a *mutual* awareness of one another. The artistic awareness must give way to another one. Reason—emotional reason—if it is to persist and not to be destroyed by the fear which lurks in self-consciousness, and makes the word a synonym for shyness, must itself become mutual. It must express itself now as the mutual self-revelation of two persons to one another. Contemplation must be replaced by communion. The artistic consciousness must give way to the religious.

Communion is the keyword of religion; and the religious impulse is the fundamental impulse of

61

reason—the impulse to communion. Let us forget about God for the moment. He won't mind, He is much too reasonable! What would you think of a father who wanted his children always to be thinking about him? Surely that he was the complete egoist! So true is it that our emotional subjectivity insists on fashioning God in our likeness. I want you rather to think of religion as a human activity, as something that men do because they are men and not animals— something that expresses that demand of our nature to achieve the capacity to live in terms of the real world outside us, not in terms of our own impulses. Then we will see that from our side religion is the pressure to live in terms of the reality of persons who are not ourselves; the craving of our reason to recognize and unite with reason in the world outside us; the urge to enter into full mutual relationship with other persons. It is the expression of our capacity as persons to know the reality of personality that is not our own, and to be known by persons in our own personal reality. It is the expression of our need to live in that knowledge; to live in the mutuality of communion.

Religion, therefore, is reason in human nature creating the community of persons—recognizing and achieving the unity of all personal life. It is the force which creates friendship, society, community, co-operation in living. That is why I am wont to say that friendship is the fundamental religious fact in human life. That capacity for communion, that capacity for entering into free and equal personal relations, is the thing that makes us human; it is the rock on which personality is built. If it were not for this we would not be human beings. It is evidenced at the lower level by the capacity to speak; to use language for the sharing of our experience; and at the highest level in the recognition by the intuition of reason that God is Love.

You will see at once from this that the reason which expresses itself in religion is primarily emotional reason. For it is based upon and it is impossible apart from the artistic reason which recognizes the significance, reality and value of the other persons in the world. But it transcends this and completes it by the simultaneous recognition that I am one of them, and that I am recognized and appreciated by them as they are by me. For the artistic rationality 'I know' is the full expression of its contemplation; for the religious consciousness this is not enough. It must say 'I know and I am known'. The promise of the full maturity of religion in human life is put perfectly in Paul's words: 'Then shall I know even as also I am known'; and it is the close of his pæan in praise of love. It expresses the perfect and complete mutuality of communion, of mutual emotional awareness.

In primitive religion we find simply the recognition of the unity of the tribe; of all the living members, and of the living with the dead and the unborn. But with the growth of reason in man, the dim stirring of emotional reason begets a disquiet, a sense of estrangement, of exclusion from the fellowship of personal reality; it appears as a sense of impurity, of pollution, of guilt and sin. Religion expresses itself as the need for reconciliation, for atonement, for the breaking down of barriers; it becomes the cry for a mediator who will put an end to the enmity that separates finite and infinite personality, and bring them together in communion. The idea of incarnation makes its appearance—the union of God and Man in *Man*, and always in its other aspect it appears as the creation of community between men, the breaking down of barriers, the ending of strife and the fusion of enemy groups into a single community. Tribes unite into cities, cities into nations, nations into empires; and throughout history the range of effective human community increases—in depth as well as breadth. That is the religious development of mankind. Wherever you find the effort to achieve human equality, to overcome the enmities and self-interests that separate individuals and classes and nations and races, you are discovering the working of religion—of religious reason—in man. You find it, for example, at the basis of modern communism, for all its profession of atheism. You find Karl Marx describing the whole stretch of human history from the breakdown of primitive tribal communism to the establishment of universal communism—the unification of all nations and races in the community of the world—which is his apocalypse, the brotherhood of men that is to be—you find him describing the intermediate stage, as the result of the estrangement (Entfremdung) of Man from himself, from his own reality; and the establishment of communism as the reconciliation of man with himself. That is religious insight—partial and incomplete, but essentially religious. For the great negation of religion is individualism, egocentricity become a philosophy; and it is inherently atheist, however much it says 'Lord, Lord!'

That, then, is religion in human nature: the slow growth of emotional reason in us, still far from its maturity. What we call religions are only the effort to express this, to symbolize the thing we dimly feel but cannot realize in living. The failure expresses itself in the sense of estrangement between two worlds, between the natural and the supernatural, this world and another world. The development of religion to maturity will be the fusion of the two— for they are not two but one. What our childishness thinks of as another world, a supernatural world, is merely the reality of this world which is hidden from us by the imperfection of our own sensitiveness.

EDUCATION OF THE EMOTIONS

THERE IS an increasing recognition in educational circles of the urgent need for a proper training of the emotions. But there is no corresponding understanding, it seems to me, of the nature of the task, so that efforts to meet the need have a curious way of tending, in the result, to defeat their own object. The traditional methods, which are now for the most part happily superseded, or at least out of favour, have been that of a stern discipline of punishment and repression. It would be generally admitted that in its worst forms this old-fashioned discipline was barbarous, and that in principle its effects were likely to prove disastrous. The 'policeman' attitude of the teacher to the child has been largely replaced by a more humane conception. Yet there is reason to doubt whether the older attitude was not more satisfactory than some of the methods which have replaced it, particularly those which rest on an appeal to the child's 'better nature'. The older disciplinary methods, if they rested upon fear, yet

1 Reprinted from *The New Era*, June 1932.

avoided the more subtle dangers of exploiting the child's natural affection and reverence for authority.

We must agree, I think, that the training of the emotions is a disciplining of the instinctive reactions of the human animal. But the important question concerns what is meant by discipline. The first distinction we have to draw is between discipline imposed by authority, and that discipline which is discovered in experience. These are fundamentally different in kind. The distinction may be grasped more easily by reference to the intellectual life. Thought may be disciplined, as it was in mediæval times, by authority. Mediæval dogmatism said to the thinker: 'This is the truth. You must learn to think in such a way that you reach such and such conclusions. If you do not, your thinking is bad thinking, because we know that these conclusions are the true ones.' Such a discipline of thought, as we should all agree, is a repression of thought. It succeeds in securing conformity in all thinkers, and so in avoiding controversy and strife. But it does so by destroying the very springs of real thinking. Compared with this, modern scientific thought is free and undogmatic. But it is not undisciplined. It finds its discipline in the effort to know, in the spontaneous intellectual activity itself. It is disciplined by the necessity of securing a real conformity of its ideas to that which it thinks about. The result is a multiplicity of theories and conclusions, a continuous struggle between rival thinkers, a very Babel of intellectual strife. Yet we all agree that such freedom is the very life-blood of thought; and in theory, at least, we stand for the liberty of the individual to think for himself.

The difference between the two types of discipline in the emotional field is precisely the same. The discipline of authority aims at securing the repression of types of emotion that are considered improper, and fostering emotional tendencies that are laudable and good. This is no doubt possible. It makes for conformity, for frictionless social relationships, for the maintaining of tradition. But it succeeds only by destroying the free spontaneity of emotional life. Against this dogmatic authority we must set our faith in the freedom of the individual to feel for himself, to develop his own emotional gifts and graces, and to reach out towards the discovery of the value of life, not through the acceptance of standards of good feeling, nor through the imposition of intellectual conceptions of goodness upon his emotional life, but through the free exercise of his own emotional capacities. That this involves discipline is certain; but it is a discipline of a very different kind. It is the discipline which comes through the continuous effort to discover the real values in life for oneself.

Emotional education should be, therefore, a considered effort to teach children to feel for themselves;

in the same sense that their intellectual training should be an effort to teach them to think for themselves. So long as we start with the assumption that we know how people ought to feel, and that it is our business to teach our pupils to feel in that way, the less successful we are the better. We have to realize how feeble and ineffective our own emotional life is, and to realize that for that very reason our notions of what is good feeling and what is not are also feeble and probably false. Then we shall perhaps begin to discover what we can do to develop in children the rich capacity for a spontaneous emotional life which has been so stunted in ourselves. One of the first results of such a fundamental change of attitude would be, I doubt not, that we should recognize that it is as ridiculous to put the emotional training of children in the hands of teachers whose emotional life is of a low grade or poorly developed, as it is to commit their intellectual education to teachers who are intellectually unintelligent and stupid.

This is the main alteration in attitude which is needed. If we assume that we approach the question of emotional training in this spirit, we can go on to ask in detail what are the main lines along which it can be carried out. We shall then have to notice that the emotional life is inherently sensuous, and that the training of emotion is primarily an education of the senses. Most of our failure in the education of the senses arises from the fact that we look upon them from a practical point of view as instruments for the achievement of practical ends; with the result that so far as we train children at all in their sensuous life we train them to use their senses for practical purposes. The sensibility, however, is an integral part of human nature, and must be developed for its own sake. We have to train children to make their sensuous life rich and fine; to see for the sake of seeing, to hear for the sake of hearing, to smell and taste and touch for the joy of living in and through the fundamental capacities of apprehension with which they are endowed.

Such an education would aim at what William Blake once called, in a moment of inspiration, 'the refinement of sensuality'. In our cruder scientific terminology we might call it the development of sensuous discrimination and co-ordination. What makes us afraid of the manifestations of sensuous life is its crudeness and vulgarity; and that is merely the mark of its primitive, undeveloped nature. It is precisely this that a proper education of the senses must deal with. It must find means to develop the capacity of the senses to reach a level of subtle and refined discrimination in what they apprehend, and the capacity to co-ordinate the discriminations of the various senses and harmonize them with one another. Crudeness and vulgarity in the expression of emotion

71

are invariably the result of crudeness and lack of refinement in sense-perception. The suppression of such offensive expressions of emotion (which is in the main what we still aim at) makes no difference to the quality of human life. If a man's nature is crude, it must of necessity be restrained, if only for the convenience of others. But the business of education is to make such restraints unnecessary by the refinement of the nature upon which they are now imposed.

There is a direct connexion, fundamental to all life, between sensuous perception and practical activity. This connexion may be checked and thwarted up to a point; but never completely. Human life, like all life, only completes itself in the connexion of immediate apprehension with action which expresses what it has become aware of. It is in this immediacy of response in action to conscious perception that all the activities of thought inevitably fail. Intellectual intelligence can never be a substitute, therefore, for the immediacy of perceptual activity. It may enrich it by raising it to a higher level, or it may impoverish it by negation and repression. The second field therefore in the education of the emotional life is the field of spontaneous expression. The sensuous apprehension of the world for its own sake, without ulterior motives, is our emotional receptivity; and that will complete itself, if it is not frustrated, in activities which are spontaneities of emotion, activities which are performed for their own sake, and not for any end beyond them. Such expressions of emotion in activity—whether in speech or song or movement—are at first crude and indiscriminate. The business of education is not to alter their spontaneous character but to refine and subtilize them, maintaining their spontaneous character so that the development of grace and fineness in activity is still without other motive than the joy of expression. Other things being equal, fineness of expression and fineness of sensory discrimination go hand in hand, so that there are not two separate trainings requisite, but one only, in which the development of fine sensory discrimination is achieved through the effort to express what is sensuously apprehended; and the effort to develop the sensory discrimination is undertaken through the effort to express it in activity of some kind. It is not my part to determine the methods through which this is to be done. Those whose business it is to experiment with teaching methods will be able to devise such methods without much difficulty, provided they are clear in their minds what it is that they wish to develop. What it is of fundamental importance to keep in the centre of our consciousness is that the education of the emotional life, whether on the side of sensuous apprehension or of activities of expression, must have no ulterior or utilitarian motive. It is an education in spontaneity, and therefore both the awareness and the activity which it seeks to refine and cultivate are ends in themselves. We are seeking in this field to make children exquisitely aware of the world in which they live, purely for its own sake, because this constitutes an increase in the quality of life in them. We are seeking to develop a fineness of expressive activity because it is good in itself, not in any sense because of what may be achieved through it.

It is plain that when such an education reaches a certain level it becomes an education in the activities of the artist. This is the necessary issue of any proper training of the emotions. It is the development of the artistic as distinct from the scientific capacities of human nature. I can point my moral, therefore, by reference to what is wrong with such æsthetic education as is normally included in the ordinary school curriculum. It turns education in art into an intellectual or scientific activity, and becomes not a training in artistry but a training of the mind in the analysis and understanding of the artistry of others. The proper training of the æsthetic capacities is, as I have described it, a training in perception and expression, which in its full results would develop to the fullest measure of which the child is capable, his ability to be an artist; that is to say, to apprehend the

74

world finely through his own sensibility, and to express it in spontaneous activity purely for the joy of doing so.

There is no need to develop this fundamental conception further. I wish rather to draw attention to the results of a failure to educate the emotional life in this way, which is, in principle, the only way in which it can be educated. I want to indicate my opinion that to neglect this side of a child's training, or to fail in it, is to fail completely in the primary business of education.

The emotional life is not simply a part or an aspect of human life. It is not, as we so often think, subordinate, or subsidiary to the mind. It is the core and essence of human life. The intellect arises out of it, is rooted in it, draws its nourishment and sustenance from it, and is the subordinate partner in the human economy. This is because the intellect is essentially instrumental. Thinking is not living. At its worst it is a substitute for living; at its best a means of living better. As we have seen, the emotional life is our life, both as awareness of the world and as action in the world, so far as it is lived for its own sake. Its value lies in itself, not in anything beyond it which it is a means of achieving. Now, any education which is fully conscious of its function must refuse to treat human life as a means to an end. It must insist that its sole duty is to develop the inherent capacity for a full human life. All true education is education in living.

But the effect of concentrating upon the education of the intellect to the exclusion of the education of the emotional life is precisely to frustrate this purpose. Because the intellect is concerned with the means of living, the exclusive concentration upon its training, and the relegation of the emotional life to a subordinate position, can only result in making our pupils capable of determining the means to human life and very little of living it. It will inevitably create an instrumental conception of life, in which all human activity will be valued as a means to an end, never for itself. When it is the persistent and universal tendency in any society to concentrate upon the intellect and its training, the result will be a society which amasses power, and with power the means to the good life, but which has no correspondingly developed capacity for living the good life for which it has amassed the means. This is, to my mind, very obviously the state in which we now find ourselves and our European civilization. We have immense power, and immense resources; we worship efficiency and success; and we do not know how to live finely. I should trace the condition of affairs almost wholly to our failure to educate our emotional life.

Another result of this failure must be the destruction of wholeness. The intellect, because it is instrumental, can only deal with life piecemeal. It must divide and it must abstract. It is in the emotional life that the unity of personality, both its individual and its social unity, is realized and maintained. It is in emotional activity that this unity is expressed. Emotion is the unifying factor in life. The failure to develop the emotional life will therefore result in abstraction and division; in a failure to see life steadily and as a whole. When the intellect takes charge, the inevitable result is specialization, the erection of particular aspects of human activity into complete conceptions of life, the substitution of the part for the whole. A practical disintegration of life, a disjointedness in conception and in practice is the consequence. Both the individual and society will be infected with the narrow vision of the specialist, which makes balance and rhythm and wholeness unrealizable and even inconceivable. Here again our own failure to educate the emotional life shows itself in the competition of desires within us which we cannot coordinate; and in the competition of rival claims and interests, factions and nations within our society. Though circumstances have forced upon us the intellectual realization of the necessity for achieving unity and wholeness in our social life, national and international, we find ourselves incapable of achieving the unity which we so urgently and consciously need.

THE EARLY DISCIPLINE OF PERSONALITY[1]

THE QUESTION of discipline has been much canvassed of recent years in discussions of educational theory and practice. There has been a marked tendency in what we might call advanced educational circles to eliminate discipline altogether. So far as this tendency represents a recoil from the methods of the drill-sergeant, there is no cause to regret it. But merely to get rid of a bad form of discipline without putting anything in its place is a serious failure in a teacher's business. It is probably true that the attack on discipline has another motive. It is part of a widespread modern desire to escape responsibility. It arises from fear of the child or from that fear of making mistakes which is only an aspect of the fear of life itself. We have no right to throw the responsibility for its training upon the child. The responsibility is ours. Not to accept it is to fail the child.

[1] Presidential Address to The Froebel Society, January 1933. Reprinted from *Child Life*, Spring Number, 1933.

It would be useless to deny that in a world which is changing so rapidly and so fundamentally as our own, the task of the teacher, particularly in the field of discipline, is exceedingly difficult. He cannot use the traditional social forms as a standard to guide him. He has to train his pupils for life in a society of which he knows nothing because it does not yet exist. He has to train them, not to take their places in a familiar and stable social order, but to be the creators of a new social order out of the chaos which has overtaken his own. In our ignorance of that new world we can say very little about it; but there is one thing certain. Only a disciplined generation will be able to build it. Discipline is perhaps of greater importance than it has ever been.

Unfortunately in our educational debates on the subject few people have stopped to ask themselves what discipline is. The idea has come to be associated with punishment, so that when we want to talk big about punishment we call it disciplinary action. Originally the word means simply 'training', and the fact that through the development of history it has come to stand for the use of force and fear and severity is surely a symptom of a sinister degradation in our conception of education. There is something far wrong when the natural association of discipline in our minds is with efforts of repression and chastisement. It betrays a conception of human relationship dominated by the craving for power and authority. No doubt it is gratifying to our sense of superiority to have people obey us—even when they are very little people—and to be able to order them about. No doubt it is easy to persuade ourselves that it is for their own good that they should learn to submit to our will. But it is an evil attitude of mind. It supports every form of snobbishness and social inequality. It is the necessary basis of class distinction and oligarchy. It is the very essence of dictatorship and tyranny. Out of it spring the evils of militarism and imperialism. The discipline it enforces is a discipline for slavery. Surely these are the very habits of mind which we have to seek to destroy.

We are liable to think that we have got beyond this conception of discipline nowadays. It is true that in its crudest form, in which subordination was maintained through fear of a physical assault, it has disappeared. But there are subtler forms which are still very much in evidence. It is quite possible to exploit the natural emotions of children in order to secure a tyrannous control of their behaviour. The natural respect of the child for its elders and its natural gratitude to those who look after it can be used against it. Its natural affection can be played upon for the same bad end. 'Other things being equal', says J. S. Mill, 'a benevolent tyranny is worse than a malevolent one.' I sometimes think that the modern tyranny of love is more dangerous and soul-destroying than the old tyranny of fear which we pride ourselves on having rejected. It is of no use merely to change the methods by which we maintain our power. It is the desire for power itself that we have to get rid of.

This power ideal is the real basis of the intellectualism of the education we provide. Its aim is not merely to provide information, but to form habit and character by imposing ideas and beliefs. It is our own ideas and our own beliefs which we seek to impose. The discipline of the mind takes the form of forcing or persuading other people to believe what we think they ought to believe. It is a denial of freedom of thought. It is no doubt true that an education which is concerned to develop freedom of thought is slowly gaining ground. But its progress is very gradual and we have still a long way to go. At the moment there is a strong reaction at work, due I think to a widespread fear that freedom of thought may destroy the basis of social control.

The other side of this tendency is the suppression of the emotional life. The discipline of the emotions is still thought of as a necessary repression of spontaneity in order to secure conformity to established habits of feeling, that is to say, to our habits of feeling. The very idea of a training in freedom of feeling and the expression of feeling has hardly begun to find a place in our ideals. Consequently the relation between mind and body is broken and we have to have a separate discipline of the body to supplement the discipline of the mind. In this field also we are apt to take pride in the fact that we have given physical training an honourable place in our conception of education. But this physical training is again a training in subordination. Its form implies that the body is only an instrument and that the discipline of the body aims at its perfection and subordination as an instrument. The spontaneous emotional life of the individual is the true life of the body; and a discipline which aims at treating the body as an instrument for the mind to use aims at suppressing the emotional life and its natural expression. The result is that the divorce of mind and body reveals itself in a system of education which seeks to discipline the mind and the body separately and not together in the natural intimacy of their relations.

With this false idea of discipline we must contrast the true one. Discipline really involves not subordination but integration. It aims at co-ordinating all the elements in personality and creating a harmonious unity in which they all co-operate freely and without hindrance. Any human action involves the co-ordination of innumerable activities. The capacity to walk or even to stand upright involves a co-operation of muscles and nerves which has to be established gradually through training and experience. If this is true of these simple activities, how much more is it of the higher types of skill which constitute the peculiar capacities of human beings, and which in their totality we call reason. The human body and mind together contain the potentiality of the development of behaviour which is the expression of skill in action almost infinitely diverse in its variety and incredibly intricate in its mechanism. Such skilled behaviour can only be realized through discipline, through the integration of a multitude of simple capacities which are trained to act together harmoniously to a single end. To secure this integration is the essence of real discipline. Its achievement is shown in the freedom and grace of action; in its rhythmic quality; in the absence of jerkiness and effort. These are the external signs of discipline. The inner signs are the feelings of freedom and joy and ease in action which testify that all the necessary factors are co-operating harmoniously in the production of the desired effect. But we must remember that human activity is essentially a co-operation between individuals and that the discipline which will produce a human result must succeed not merely in integrating the various capacities of the individual but in integrating individuals themselves in a community of free co-operation. These are not two separate forms of discipline. They are two aspects of one and the same. It is impossible to do the one except in and through the other.

This true discipline which integrates the elements of human life in the joy of rhythmic social activity is not one which has to be imposed either through fear or through the solicitation of affection. There is a craving for it in all human nature. The longing for discipline of this kind is simply the longing to fulfil one's own nature, the longing for skill and for joy in living. Much of the evil and the suffering in social life comes from the thwarting of this desire either through maladjustments in the social and economic machinery or from the fear and greed that give rise to these. A baby's joy in learning to walk is a joy in discovering the discipline of the body on which its capacity to move about freely depends. So is a boy's joy in learning to ride a bicycle or to make a boat with a knife out of a piece of wood. Equally the joy in human companionship is the expression of a human skill achieved only through the discipline which integrates the capacities of different people and so gives rise to friendship, to the capacity to be together and to do things together freely, harmoniously and joyfully. Give this instinctive craving a chance, and human nature, especially when it is fresh and unspoiled, will respond to the call of discipline with a rush of spontaneous happiness.

Unfortunately we have our own crooked idea of

what human nature is and of how it ought to shape as it develops. This idea has its roots in our own experience and in what we are. As a result we quite sincerely try to make children grow up in our own image; or, at least in the image of what we ourselves would crookedly like to be and think we ought to be. But our ideals are hardly less crooked than ourselves. Matthias Alexander tells a story of a little girl who was permanently lopsided and who was brought to him for treatment. After working with her for some time he managed to get her to stand quite straight. Then he asked her to walk across to her mother. She walked perfectly straight for the first time in her life and then, bursting into tears, threw herself into her mother's arms, crying: 'Oh, Mummy, I'm all crooked!' In much the same way we feel straight, not when we are really straight but when we have become thoroughly accustomed to our own crookedness; and in the name of uprightness we impose our crookedness upon the children for their own good.

There are certain implications of this conception of discipline which I must mention. It demands, in the first place, the integration, throughout all life, of theory and practice. Activity, which is the expression of skill, is primary. Theory is for the sake of action. Knowledge is a means to life, not an end in itself. The failure to recognize this and the consequent failure to integrate theory and practice all along the line is still the main defect in our theory and practice of education. Knowledge which is not learned in and through its application; knowledge which makes no immediate and recognized contact with action and life, is worse than useless. It is at once meaningless and an impediment.

The integration of theory and practice is impossible unless we recognize that the body and the life of the body are not subordinate. Our bodies are not merely instruments for the mind to use. If we think they are we banish beauty altogether, for beauty is essentially sensuous and physical. If we treat the body as an instrument, its skill in action becomes utilitarian, a means to achieve ends set for it by the mind. But the highest forms of skill exhibit themselves in action which is its own end; and the beauty and expressiveness of such action is its own supreme value. It is the mind that is instrumental. Hence it follows that true discipline must begin with the education of sensibility. The senses have their own life and the activity of the senses is part of the good life and essential to all good living. Life is action and life is good only when action is a joy. Action, in turn, is a joy only when it is free, and freedom in action has its basis in an integrating discipline and its expression in grace, loveliness and charm. These things are impossible except where the action itself is a source of joy to the agent. When we learn to see things for the joy of seeing them; to hear and touch because it is good to hear and touch, we have begun to live naturally, and human nature is so constructed that the body responds spontaneously to such a use of the senses, with action which expresses and translates what it apprehends with pleasure, into activities which are themselves lovely to see and to hear and to share. That is why I insist that the education of sensibility is the basis of education and the basis of all true discipline.

Finally, I should like to stress still further the social aspect of the discipline of personality. The integration of individuals in society is not something added to the integration of elements in the individual person. It is really another aspect of the same thing. The reason for this is that personality is something that only exists between people and which cannot exist in the individual in isolation. It is impossible to integrate an individual person in isolation. The creation of harmonious relationships between children so that the joy of skilful and disciplined co-operation develops is the primary condition of the development of the individual himself. Without this integration of individuals in community and co-operation, no other form of discipline and training is possible which will result in the proper integration of individual capacities. Instead of a training *for* society what is required from the beginning is a training *in* society in which children learn the capacity for rhythmic co-operation. The acquirement of that skill results in grace and joy in common activities and so in the capacity for freedom in the community of friendship. Nor is this integration of individuals in the personal unity of a social life something distinct from the interplay between the individual and his work—co-operation with matter. The complete integration which is the aim and expression of true discipline lies in the communal use of the world we live in for the increase and perfecting of human joy in life.

Out of these considerations there emerge certain general principles which apply directly to the early discipline of personality.

1. True discipline is a process of integration and co-ordination, never of repression.

2. All true discipline is the discipline of personality, and therefore the integration and co-ordination of the elements of personality.

3. Such discipline results in skill and grace in action. It is felt and expressed in joy. It is rhythm and harmony in the activities of living.

4. Discipline is the fundamental demand of the human heart, without which it cannot be satisfied. Therefore, if a child persistently refuses discipline there is something wrong with the discipline.

5. We do not know what is good for ourselves. How then can we know what is good for a child?

But we can all recognize joy and loveliness when we see it. There, then, lies the test of our practice.

6. An integrated personality implies the creation of community between individuals. Therefore, all discipline is communal.

7. Personality is inherently creative. Children, therefore, are not material to be moulded. They are potential creators of society. We must treat them as such.

8. Joy in living is the end of life. All skills are subordinate to this rule.

In conclusion we must remember that the foundations of this development of disciplined community can only be laid properly in early life. The process of integration has its own laws of development by which we must abide. Children must grow into wholeness and the business of early education is to provide carefully and fully for this natural growth in the integration of the natural capacities. The early discipline of personality has to lay the foundations for the development of interdependence and co-operation in joy among all the elements of personality and between children. It is a training in rhythmic co-operation, in doing things that it is a joy to do together, not in learning things that may possibly come in useful later on. It is a great task but not a difficult one; provided that we are prepared to follow nature and subordinate ourselves to nature. The difficulties mostly arise through the attempt to frustrate and thwart the natural processes in order to realize some unnatural ideal.

THE PERSONAL LIFE[1]

I HAVE BEEN asked in this address to provide a
background for a conference which is to be concerned with Sex Problems, particularly as they affect
women. In order to do that I have chosen to discuss
with you the general question of the personal life.
It seems to me that most of our discussions about sex
and our attempts to deal with the problems which
it raises, are vitiated by our failure to see it in its
proper setting. If it were not for the close relation
that exists between sex and the whole form of our
lives as human beings, there would be very little
difficulty in dealing with it. It is for this reason that
the background is so important. Let me try to explain
what I mean by this.

In the first place, we must be clear about what we
mean by the personal life. It is the life we live as
human beings. That might seem to include everything, and, in a sense, it does. But there is a central

[1] Opening Address at a conference on the Changing
Moral Standard, May 4th, 1934. Reprinted from
Health & Empire, June 1934.

core of our life which is personal in a special sense, and through which all the rest *may* take on a special character that makes it personal. It is with this central core of personal life that I am concerned, and we can distinguish it most easily by contrasting it with other aspects which are not in this primary sense personal. There are, in particular, two terms in common use from which we must distinguish it. We talk of social life and we talk of individual life. Personal life is neither the one nor the other.

The habit, which we have inherited from several centuries of individualism, of talking about human life in terms of a contrast between the individual and society is a very misleading one. When we think of society we think primarily of the State and of men and women as citizens of the State, subject to the restrictions which it imposes upon our freedom to do as we please. We think, secondarily, of the web of custom and tradition in which we are enmeshed and which, by a more subtle pressure, cuts across our individual tendencies and compels us to conform to ways of living which are conventional. What is common to both these conceptions of society and the social life is the existence of an organization which we ourselves do not make, and which is stronger than we, which dictates to us how we must behave. We can see that this social organization to which we must conform is necessary, because we have to live together in such a way as will avoid the open clash of differences of individual character, impulse, and purpose. We have to live as members of groups. We have to co-operate with one another, very often with numbers of people whom we do not know or do not like, for common purposes. And some generally accepted scheme to which we all conform, whether it is enforced by law or merely maintained by custom and public opinion, is absolutely inevitable. Life, except in the wilderness, would be impossible without it. For all that, it often cuts across our private inclinations and thwarts our individual desires. It destroys our freedom in such cases, and if the tension is sufficiently strong it may frustrate us completely as individuals and force us to a lifelong acquiescence in ways of living which seem to us meaningless and futile.

Through this experience we come to contrast the individual and society, and to think of those corners of our lives which escape from the control of law and custom as peculiarly our own, because in them we can live through our own individual impulses and fulfil our private purposes. And we are apt to identify this field of free individual living with our personal life. This is the first mistake against which I want to warn you. It is a half-truth, and therefore more dangerous than a complete falsehood. The personal life is not the life that we live in solitude, when there is nobody to interfere with our personal preferences and prejudices. We are not particularly personal in our baths. Hermits and castaways on desert islands have tried that way to the freedom of the personal life without very conspicuous success.

The personal life is essentially a life of relations between people. It is, in a sense, social life, and all its peculiar problems—and they are the subtlest and most difficult that we are faced with—are problems of human relationships. But it is not social in the sense in which we ordinarily use the term. All of us know how a piece of social activity, like the smooth running of a club or the satisfactory working of a committee, can be ruined by the intrusion of personal differences between its members. The difficulties of the personal life make social life impossible. It is this difference between personal life and social life that we must get clear. They are obviously not the same thing, because it would seem that a certain degree of impersonality, a willingness to overlook and to suppress the peculiarly personal elements in our relationships with one another is essential to social life. If we all insist on being personal we shall soon bring social activities to a sorry end. Think what this means. The satisfactory working of social life depends upon entering into relationships with other people, not with the whole of ourselves but only with part of ourselves. It depends on suppress-

ing, for the time being at least, the fullness and wholeness of our natures. It is this, perhaps, which makes
us identify the personal life with the individual life.
We often feel that only when we are free from any
necessity of co-operation, or even of relationship,
with other people, can we be wholly ourselves. But
this is an illusion, because to be ourselves at all we
need other people. When we are alone we haven't
even the opportunity of expressing ourselves in
speech. And that, with all that it implies, is a very
essential part of our whole selves.

This enables us to see at least what the personal
life demands. It demands a relationship with one
another in which we can be our whole selves and
have complete freedom to express everything that
makes us what we are. It demands a relationship
with one another in which suppression and inhibition
are unnecessary. The personal life is, at any rate, that
part of our life in which we are seeking this, however
much we may fail to find it or to achieve it. There
are, then, two very different ways in which we can
enter into relations with our fellows. We can, in the
first place, associate with others in order to achieve
some purpose that we all share. Out of this there
springs a life of social co-operation through which we
can provide for our common needs, and achieve
common ends. We may define this social life in terms
of purposes. That is its great characteristic. There is

in this field always a reason beyond the mere association for associating and co-operating in that particular way. Because of this we cannot enter into this form of relationship with the whole of ourselves as complete persons, because the purpose is always only one of our purposes. There are others which cannot be achieved by that particular association. We cannot, therefore, live a personal life on the basis of such relationships. The whole complex of activities which are generated in this way is what we mean usually by society or by social life. But there is a second way in which we can enter into relationships with one another. We may associate purely for the purpose of expressing our whole selves to one another in mutuality and fellowship. It is difficult to find a word to express this kind of relationship which will convey its full meaning, not because there are no words, but because they have all been specialized and degraded by misuse. Friendship, fellowship, communion, love, are all in one way or another liable to convey a false or partial meaning. But what is common to them all is the idea of a relationship between us which has no purpose beyond itself; in which we associate because it is natural for human beings to share their experience, to understand one another, to find joy and satisfaction in living together; in expressing and revealing themselves to one another. If one asks why people form friendships or love one another, the question is simply unanswerable. We can only say, because it is the nature of persons to do so. They can only be themselves in that way. It is this field of human relations which constitutes what we call the personal life, and that is the right name for it. Because that is the only way in which we can live as persons at all, the only form of human life in which we can be our whole selves or our essential selves without self-suppression and self-mutilation.

Perhaps it would clarify this fundamental issue if I took particular and concrete instances. Think first of a Trade Union. It is an association of a very fundamental kind. It brings men together in co-operation for a purpose which goes to the very roots of social life. It can even command loyalties which its members may be prepared to defend to the death against other forms of social organization. But it is not a personal association. Its basis is a common purpose, and because of this its members enter it in virtue of one particular aspect of their humanity. They are not members because they are human beings but because they have a special economic interest in common with all the others. This gives an exclusive character to the association, because only individuals who share that particular interest are qualified for membership. But it also, for the same reason, restricts the range of human interest which the association serves, for all its members have other interests which cannot be served by the Trade Union. That is what I mean in saying that men do not enter into such associations as persons, with the whole of themselves.

It is important to realize that all organized relationships are of this kind, even if the organization is not enforced by explicit laws or rules of membership but only by custom or public opinion. Wherever in human association you have organization you have a group which exists for a purpose, and which, therefore, cannot include people as persons but only as people who happen to have that particular purpose or interest. It is, for example, characteristic of the State that it cannot be on a basis of personal membership. Men and women are members of one State or another as citizens because they have interests which they do not share with the members of other States. A citizen is something considerably lower than a person, because citizenship is only one limited aspect of a person.

Now, contrast this with a personal relationship or association, a friendship for example, between two men or two women. If the two people are associated merely for what they can get out of one another it obviously is not a friendship. Two people are friends because they love one another. That is all you can say about it. If the relationship had any other reason for it we should say that one or other of them was pretending friendship from an ulterior motive. This means in effect that friendship is a type of relationship into which people enter as persons with the whole of themselves. To ask David what he expects to get out of his friendship with Jonathan is to insult him by suggesting that he only associates with his friend from self-interest. No doubt he might answer that he gets everything that makes life worth living; but of course what he means is that he gets friendship out of it, which is exactly what he puts into it. This is the characteristic of personal relationships. They have no ulterior motive. They are not based on particular interests. They do not serve partial and limited ends. Their value lies entirely in themselves and for the same reason transcends all other values. And that is because they are relations of persons as persons. They are the means of living a personal life.

Now we understand what the personal life is in distinction both from the individual and the social life. It is the life which we live as persons, and we can live it only by entering into relationships with other people on a fully personal basis, in which we give ourselves to one another; or, to put the same thing the other way round, in which we accept one another freely for what we are, and in which therefore there is and can be no purpose other than the sharing of our lives in fellowship. The impulse to do this is simply the impulse to be ourselves completely; not to gain anything, not to achieve anything, or to do anything in particular, but simply to be ourselves as fully and completely as is possible. Now we have only to state this and grasp it to realize that the whole significance of human life is to be found here. What other significance can our existence have than to be ourselves fully and completely? Obviously none. In the nature of things this must include in some way everything else. The social life and the individual life can only be subordinate to this. They are necessary as a basis for this. In other words, the whole network of organized human association has only one meaning: that it is the necessary foundation on which the personal life can be built. Society exists for the life of personal relationship. Personal life does not exist for society. To think it does is to try to stand the world on its head.

Before coming to the special case with which we are concerned, personal relations between men and women, I should like to add a few further remarks about this all-important distinction between social life and personal life. All associations of people which are not personal are functional. I mean by this that the place of the individual is determined by his function in the group, by the particular service which he renders to the general purpose of the whole. From the point of view, for example, of the economic organization of society, people are not primarily persons but individuals performing a specific economic function. They are doctors, or shoemakers, or coal-miners, and so forth. And their relations to one another are the relations of these functions. They are not personal relations. These functional relationships depend upon differences of skill and capacity for different tasks. And the problem of organizing society properly depends upon getting square pegs in square holes and round pegs in round holes. The basis for it is the natural differences between people which fit them for different tasks and different services to the community. From that point of view it is obvious and necessary that people should not be equal—that is to say, that there should be, as there obviously are, great differences of natural quality and capacity between people. But when we turn to the personal life we are in a different world. There is no inherent reason why a personal relationship should be based upon these natural functional differences. Because personal relationships are relationships of persons as persons, their functional differences have nothing directly to do with the relationship, though they may have a great deal to do with its quality and character and the ways in which it expresses itself. It is just nonsense to say that people of different races, or different professions, or different nationalities, or different sexes, cannot be friends. Of course they can, and are. Personal relationships override all the distinctions which differentiate people. Personal relationship is possible between any two persons because it is based purely on the fact that they are both persons. It may be difficult in some cases and easy in other cases. It may be fuller in some cases and more meagre in others. But it is universally possible. An Englishman may refuse to be friends with an Indian, but that is a matter of choice. It is not an impossibility. In this sense all persons are equal; and this is the first law of the personal life. It does not mean that there are not immense differences between one person and another; it means that these differences have no bearing upon the possibility of personal relationships and have nothing do to with the structure or the constitution of the personal life. On the other hand, it does not mean that these differences can be ignored or should be overlooked in the personal life. The differences remain, and become the basis of the infinite variety of experience which can be shared in the life of personal relationship. When two people become friends they establish between themselves a relation of equality. They meet as equals, as man to man. There is and can be no functional subservience of one to the other. One cannot be the superior and the other the inferior. If the relation is one of inequality, then it is just not a personal relationship. But once a personal relationship is established the differences between the persons concerned are the stuff out of which the texture of their fellowship is woven. And provided the equal relationship is maintained, it is precisely the differences that enrich the relationship. The greater the differences the more there is to share. The greater the fundamental differences between two persons are the more difficult it is to establish a fully personal relation between them, but also the more worth while the relation will be if it can be established and maintained. All great things are difficult, and this is the greatest of all.

I shall make one other point only. The personal life is the field of freedom. That means more than that people ought to be free in their personal lives. It means that without freedom there is and can be no personal life at all. It means that the measure of our freedom and the measure of our personal life are one and the same. The institutional life of society never can be free, as I have shown you. We must always be less than ourselves in it. It exists only through the imposition of restraints, even if they are self-imposed. It can be the *means* to freedom in the real life, that is, the personal life, if it is properly related to it and is built to serve it. The personal life is, on the contrary, just that life in which we are seeking freedom in our relations with one another. It is that central core of our experience in which we are seeking to accept one another and to be accepted for what we are, so that we may be ourselves and express ourselves for one another. And that is freedom. Freedom is what we seek, and what if we are successful we find, in all those relations in which we treat one another as equals for no reason but to be ourselves together. It is only in such a way that we can live spontaneously in the free and full expression of what we are, without constraint.

Such an understanding of the difference between social life and personal life; such a comprehension of the two very different types of relationship that always co-exist between human beings, is the only background against which the problems of sex can be reasonably discussed and dealt with. For the difference of sex between men and women, fundamental and unchangeable though it is, is only one of those natural differences which provide the inexhaustible variety and richness of the personal life. Unless we begin by recognizing that in the nature of things the personal life is the primary aspect of human life, and that the functional relationships of the social life are in their nature subordinate and gain their human significance only through their subordination to the personal life, we shall be defeated at the outset. We shall never begin to understand our problem. Unless we remember always that institutions are for persons and not persons for institutions; unless we hold fast to the truth that the Sabbath is made for man, not man for the Sabbath, we had better not meddle with the problem of sex relationship either in theory or in practice. The full relationship between a man and a woman is a personal relationship. It is a relation between two persons who happen to be of opposite sexes. The sexual relationship, on the other hand, taken by itself, is an organic, functional relationship which we share with plants and animals; and from the social point of view it is an institutional relationship, a central element in the functioning of the *social* life.

Against this background we can formulate the one question that is of fundamental importance about the problem of sex. Are we to regard the question of the relation of the sexes as a problem of the personal life or not? The issue lies there. You will probably want to answer at once: 'Of course it is a problem of the personal life; there can be no doubt about that.' I am in entire agreement. But I wonder whether you have thought out the implications of that affirmation. Until quite recently societies have all denied it, and in practice they deny it still. They insist on treating it as an institutional question primarily. They look upon it as primarily a question of the functional relationships of the sexes in society. I do not deny that this is an aspect of the question; but if the question is a personal question at all, then this aspect cannot be primary but must be subordinate.

The personal life cannot be subordinated to the social life without destroying its basis. One of the effects of our traditional habit of treating it as primarily a social question is that we do not possess the rudiments of a sexual morality. For morality is the principle of the personal life, and, as we have seen, the personal life is neither social nor individual. Consequently, sex, in its essence, is neither a social question nor an individual question, but a personal one. Sex problems are problems in the relations of persons.

But what are the plain implications of this affirmation? The first is that our primary consideration cannot be to maintain marriage and the family. These are social institutions. They may be good institutions, they may be necessary institutions, but that is not the point. They are institutions. They belong to the social or functional aspect of life. Therefore they cannot be the things of primary consideration in dealing with personal relations. If you approach the problem of the relation of the sexes with the attitude that the primary consideration is to maintain marriage and the family at all costs; if you think that this is the touchstone for testing all proposals and all solutions; if you believe that the relationship of the sexes must be judged by reference to its effect upon these institutions, then you are denying that sex belongs to the personal life. You are proposing to act as if persons existed for the sake of institutions. And it is not true.

It is contrary to the natural order. It is profoundly immoral.

I want to make this quite clear, and to leave no room for misapprehension. I am not attacking marriage or the family. Neither am I defending them. I am only insisting that they are institutions, and that therefore they exist for the sake of the personal life. They must therefore be judged, both in general and in each particular case, by their effect upon the freedom that is fundamental to the moral life of personality. It may be true that under proper social conditions the institution of monogamous marriage is the social form of the relation of the sexes which best provides for the freedom of personal life between men and women. But this cannot be taken for granted, particularly in a form of society which is so improper and unnatural as our own. I mean that we must leave the institutional aspect to take care of itself while we concentrate our attention upon the primary personal aspect. For surely, if marriage and the family are the natural and proper social forms of the relations of the sexes, then if the personal relations of men and women are right they will express themselves naturally through those forms. If, on the other hand, marriage and the family, as we know them, are not the natural forms in which the true moral relationships of men and women would express themselves, any attempt to maintain these forms through legal or social pressure can only result in betraying the personal life, in perverting morality, and in poisoning and ultimately destroying the very institutions that we are seeking to preserve. Anyone who really believes in marriage and the family will never get excited about the danger of their breaking down or being destroyed. Above all, he will never attempt to maintain them by legal or economic pressure. That would be a sign that he really believed that they were unnatural and that he had ulterior motives in his mind. If these institutions are the eternal natural forms of the sex relations in human life, and if in our own society they are showing a tendency to be frustrated or repudiated by large numbers of people, then there is only one conclusion to be drawn. It is that there is something far wrong with the social order in which we live. There must be social conditions which are perverting the natural expression of the personal life. The conclusion will be that our social order calls for a drastic reconstruction in the interests of morality.

Let us, then, leave this subordinate question aside and attend to the really important one. We are concerned to discover the principles which do govern and should govern the personal relations of men and women to one another. If this is really what we are concerned about we need not remain in doubt. We have discovered the two main principles already.

They are expressed in the ideas of freedom and equality. A personal relation is a relation of equality, and it exists for the realization and expression of freedom. There is no question whether men and women should treat one another as equals, or seek freedom in their relations. These are the conditions of any true personal relationship. They are the definitions of the structure of the personal life. The only question is how that equality and that freedom can be secured and maintained. But you must remember that we cannot lay down rules for this. Rules to be observed are, of course, restrictions upon freedom. Freedom means freedom, not something else; and to live freely means to live not by rules but spontaneously. The real question is one about the conditions under which freedom and equality can actually be realized. What we have to do is to seek out and get rid of the obstacles which prevent equality and freedom from existing in the relationships of men and women to one another.

The first set of conditions is social. No political or economic form, no social institution however hoary with ancient associations, has any value in itself. It is a means to an end. The organization of life can only be justified if it makes possible the equality and freedom of human beings in the personal life. When an institution becomes a fetter upon freedom and begins to frustrate the personal life it becomes a festering sore in the body of humanity. To retain it unchanged is, *then*, a social wickedness. I am convinced that the main source of our difficulties about the relation of the sexes lies in the social structure of our civilization. The nature of our economic and legal organization makes it exceedingly difficult for men and women to meet on a basis of freedom and equality. Until these conditions are changed our sex problems will prove insoluble. Until we can make up our minds to reorganize our societies on the principle that men and women are persons, free and equal; until we give effect to that principle by producing the social conditions that would make it possible for us to behave freely as equals, all our social efforts to deal with the sex problem are mere palliatives, mere soothing ointments applied to the symptoms of a deep-seated disease.

The second set of conditions belongs to the personal field. We have to discover and to develop in ourselves and in our social tradition a true moral attitude to sex. This is, in a sense, the core of the problem. I do not believe that if you create proper social and economic conditions everything else will come right of itself. I do believe, on the other hand, that unless you deal with these external conditions you cannot develop a true moral attitude to anything. Indeed, the effort to construct a true and just order of society is the main part of the effort to create a true moral outlook. The two things are intimately bound up. Those people who try strenuously to develop moral and religious ideals in the community without altering the conditions of life are trying to make bricks without straw. This is particularly true with regard to sex, because of the intimate way in which the problems of sex are bound up in our tradition with the problems of property. But even if by a miracle we could suddenly produce proper social and economic conditions, we should still have the inner problem to deal with. It would, however, be a natural problem, not an impossible problem. And human nature solves its problems with zest when the natural conditions for the solution are provided.

What, then, is the moral problem of sex? It is the problem of subordinating the functional relation of the sexes to their relation as persons. It is the problem of taking the sexual aspect of life up into the personal aspect and making it one of the differences between persons through which their personal life in relation to one another is enriched. It is this that we find so difficult. We seem unable to regard sex as part and parcel of the normal personal life. We are so afraid of it that we try to keep it apart. We do not wish to recognize it. So, when a man and a woman meet, they either behave to one another as if the difference of sex was non-existent, or else they are so aware of the difference that other considerations are crowded out. The only solution is one which breaks down this choice between two exclusive attitudes and enables us at once to accept and rejoice in the difference, while recognizing it as only one element in the relationship of two free and equal persons. Morality depends, in this relationship as in all others, on our ability to treat one another always as persons, and the differences between us as the means for realizing and expressing and enjoying our common personality. In this the whole solution is contained.

I have been concerned only with the background to the discussions of the concrete and practical problems with which you are concerned. May I, in closing, try to put in a word the practical issue which I have been seeking to formulate. There is one general question which we have to settle first. Which of two things do we consider the more important, that men and women should be prevented from having sexual relations except under certain conditions determined by law and social custom, or to make possible the full development of the personal life? The answer you give to this choice determines completely the attitude of mind in which you will approach and deal with all the particular problems. I have no doubt of my own answer. It is that the development of the personal life of humanity must take precedence of all merely social and institutional demands. I ask, therefore, that men and women should have complete freedom to enter into personal relations on a basis of absolute equality, and that the social conditions which could make this possible should be established. All that this means is that we recognize the right of men and women, just as men and women, to become friends and to develop their friendship in the way that it demands, without pressure or interference from without. It means that we should allow them to discover in experience the moral conditions under which friendship is possible. They cannot be discovered in any other way. If you say that this is to give a charter to immorality I can only reply that it is precisely the opposite. It is to accept the basic principle of morality. If you say: 'But in many cases it will mean that people who are not married will have sexual relations', I can only reply that in the interests of morality we must take the risk of that. For what is the alternative? It is simply that we should seek to prevent the development of the personal life, that is to say, the moral life of freedom and equality, between men and women altogether. And that, I submit, is no solution at all. History has proved it.

THE VIRTUE OF CHASTITY

M Y TASK in this lecture is not to defend any recognized view of sex morality, either orthodox
or unorthodox. I shall come to no definite conclusions
about the questions that people are asking so insist-
ently nowadays about marriage and divorce and free
love and so on. I want to do something, if I can, much
more honest and, therefore, much more valuable.
I want to try to understand and to try to help you a
little to understand.

On such a subject this is very difficult; because it is
very difficult to be honest or even to know whether
you are being honest or not. Prejudice and bias, the
heat of unreal emotions generated by associations of
ideas, are everywhere—in ourselves. The very words
we have to use are tainted and spoiled by overtones of
feeling which blind us. So I must ask you to be
patient with me and with yourselves; not to expect
me to answer questions to which I do not know the
answer, nor to undertake the defence or the destruction of positions of which I am not sure.

Our greatest need is for a deep inner sincerity that

will not let us plead a case which we should like to see prevail. I shall try—I cannot promise to succeed in this—to be sincere; to say what I think, leaning on experience rather than on logical argument; and to tell you when I feel convinced, when I feel that I can only reach a balance of probabilities, and when I am guessing and groping in the dark.

I shall begin with one thing of which I feel quite sure. The problem of the relations between men and women with which we are faced in modern civilization is an urgent one and a new one. It is perhaps the most important of all the problems which this generation is called upon to face. But it is also a new problem in the history of civilization. Many people fail to see this, and it is vitally important to recognize it.

The development of civilization depends on the interplay of two factors, individual initiative and social cohesion. If the forces which maintain social cohesion manage to overcome individual initiative civilization stagnates and deteriorates. If the forces making for individual independence and initiative—for individualism, in fact—become overmastering, they disrupt social unity and produce a catastrophe. Roughly speaking, the intellect is on the side of individualism, while emotion is on the side of unity.

Now, it is roughly true that when civilization began to develop, it was through the rise of individuals standing out from the mass who showed the capacity to act and think for themselves and so to become spear-heads of initiative. That development of individuals has gone on with increasing speed and effect. But it has been until recently almost completely confined to men. We might say with very great truth that when men took to being individuals —in thinking and fighting, and inventing, and creating—women took charge of the maintenance of social unity. So the sexes were differentiated in their social functions—man towards individuality and intellect, woman towards unity and emotion. These, of course, are rough statements, but sufficiently correct for their purpose.

It is this specialization of the sexes which has governed the social organization of marriage and the family, and so determined our sex-morality. When people say that 'woman's place is the home', this is, in fact, what they mean. To allow men to specialize, assert their individual initiative, and stand on their achievements as individuals, women must guard the inner springs of personal unity and love. Of all the great thinkers of Europe until nearly our own time, Plato was the only one who dared to challenge that differentiation of the sexes with a full knowledge of what it might mean—the extinction of the family as the focus of social unity.

In our own day, however, it has been challenged

with increasing success, not in theory but practically. Women have increasingly insisted that they too are individuals, and must be permitted to stand upon their own achievement; to realize their own capacities as individuals; to exercise their own initiative in the development of civilization. They have entered the world of literature and art, of politics, of the professions, of industry and commerce. And this is, I think, bound to continue and increase. We cannot do other than look upon it as a momentous advance in culture and civilization; and to be afraid of it is surely to fail in faith and courage. But it means in principle the disappearance of a differentiation of function which has governed the relation of the sexes from the dawn of history. No longer can we look to women to guard the delicate spiritual attitudes which maintain the unity of persons in the face of the differentiating forces of individualism—of private self-realization. No longer can men specialize in the intellectual life while women specialize in the emotional. The social unity—which is necessarily a matter of emotion—must be maintained, if we are not to perish, but it can no longer be maintained through the differentiation of the social functions of the sexes. Women, if they are to develop their intellectual initiative will necessarily demand the right to stand side by side with men as equal, independent individuals. That is the crisis we are facing. That is why

I insist that *our* problem of sex-morality is a new one in the history of civilization, and not to be solved by any insistence on traditional forms of social organization.

There is, however, one assumption which I make, and cannot help making. It is that in trying to find a clue to the reconstruction of social relations between men and women under the new circumstances we must approach it as members of a Christian tradition. To abandon Christianity would be to turn out the light before beginning our search. Do not imagine, however, that this means that we must declare ourselves upholders of so-called 'Christian views'. I am strongly of opinion that most of our so-called 'Christian' morality, particularly in the field of sex, has little fundamental relationship to the outlook and spirit of the founder of Christianity. Let me try and explain what I mean. The orthodox European morality—usually called Christian—is intellectual and, therefore, external. It is a matter of rule or principle applied to the organization of life. Take first its externality. When we say that a man and woman are 'living in sin' or have 'immoral relations', what do we mean? We mean simply that they are living together without being married. Now, marriage is a social institution, that is to say, a generally recognized arrangement involving a contract between two people. It is constituted by a promise made before witnesses that they will confine their sexual relationships to one another. The making of that contract confers upon them the right to have sexual intercourse, and makes such intercourse not immoral. Now, to use the existence of such a contract as a test of morality is to use an external standard. That is all we are concerned with at the moment. On such a ground the virtue of chastity consists in refraining from all sexual experience except within the institution of marriage. To say that sex-relationships are moral *because* a man and woman are married, immoral *because* they are not married, is to base morality upon something external.

But, you will say, there is much more in it than this. Undoubtedly there is. But before we go deeper let me remind you of the enormous extent to which we do use this external test, and nothing more, in our moral judgments, and of the strength of the feelings which are aroused and calmed by merely applying the external test. What, then, does lie behind? A moral principle. It is a matter of moral principle for us that the sex-life should be confined within marriage, and within monogamous marriage. That is, I think, the proper way to put it, instead of saying that our principle is one of sexual fidelity. Because if a man and woman lived together in perfect fidelity without being married, the European tradition and conscience would still insist that they were guilty of immorality, though when pressed we might have difficulty in justifying our feeling on moral grounds. I cannot help feeling that though when we reflect and try to justify our judgments to ourselves on grounds of principle, we feel bound to go deeper than marriage as an institution, yet in the main it is the external fact—married or not married—that controls our practical judgments and our practical conduct.

Let us grant the principle, then, without further enquiry. Now, any principle is an intellectual thing. It is a universal judgment upon which we base our conduct. It is a rule defining how we ought to behave; and we apply it in particular cases to approve or forbid particular actions. A morality based on principle, therefore, is a morality based on thought, on judgment, on laws governing conduct and determining intellectually what is right and what is wrong. Such a morality is based on *will*; and I want to draw your attention to the idea of *will* and its implications. The idea of will originated with the Stoics. It turns upon the idea of a struggle between reason and the passions. For the Stoics passion, impulse, desire—the emotions in the widest sense—were the source of evil. To live rightly was to dominate the emotional life by reason, and so to act by will; that is to say, in the way that you have rationally decided to act, whether you want to or not. Now that opposition between will and impulse has gone deeply into our

European moral tradition. Stoicism was the dominating philosophy of Rome. It made Roman law. And the Roman tradition, which is by far the strongest element in European civilization, is a Stoic tradition. It lies at the root of our moral conscience, particularly as regards sex. The mediæval idea of chastity, which went so far as to identify chastity with complete lifelong sexual abstinence, is pure Stoicism. Sexual desire is held to be in itself evil; and 'virtue' consists in dominating and suppressing it on principle, by force of will, in a lifelong struggle. We have given that up in its extreme form, though I think there is far more of it in our attitude to sex still than we dare or care to acknowledge. But we still retain the main idea—that morality means the control of desire by reason; suppression of inclination in favour of purpose, i.e. of action willed in accordance with rational decisions. This yields us the idea of duty— the distinction between what we ought to do and what we want to do. Indeed, Kant—the greatest of our European moralists—rested his whole moral theory upon the clear-cut distinction between acting from inclination and acting from duty; and identified will, which is the source of dutiful action, with practical reason.

I need not argue this further. I think you will agree with me that what we call 'Christian' morality, at least in the field of sex, does mean the control of emotion by principle, signifies the capacity to say 'no', on grounds of rational principle, to desire and emotion, and so depends upon will for the suppression of emotion as the source of action. For 'Christian' morality, in sex, the right thing to do is to bring our emotions and desires under the control of principle and harness them to the service of universal purposes. Intellect, that is to say, not emotion, is the governing source of good conduct, particularly in regard to sex. That is what is ultimately meant by saying that morality is a matter of principle.

I hope that this has made clear what I meant when I said that the orthodox European tradition of sex-morality, what we refer to as 'Christian' morality, is essentially external and intellectual. It is external *because* it is intellectual, for the intellect is essentially external, objective, outward looking, dealing with external situations and the external world, and so *organizing* life in terms of external situations. But that point I have no time to elaborate. Rather let me call your attention at once to the fact that what Jesus did was to substitute an inner and emotional basis of behaviour for an external and intellectual one. It was the externality of the Pharisee morality which he condemned. And his basis for morality was not rules, principles or laws, but love. And love is emotional, not intellectual. We are driven to the conclusion that our so-called 'Christian' morality is not Christian at all in the true sense, but Stoic, and that this is particularly true in our morality of sex. The true Christian morality will be quite different from our orthodox one in its basis and in its outlook. It will be emotional and in terms of love; not intellectual and in terms of purposes and principles.

Now, of course, our orthodox sex-morality does relate love and marriage very closely, and we do insist that love is the only proper basis for marriage. In that case are we not being unfair to the orthodox position? On the whole I think we are not, because I think that on the whole this common insistence on love is neither very effective nor very sincere. In fact it is largely sentimentalism. I must give you some of my reasons for thinking so.

In the first place, the love that is looked for is neither considered in itself moral or immoral, but a passion; something that happens or does not happen between two people; an instinctive and violent attraction. It is not considered the real basis of morality. It may be beautiful, natural, a source of joy and delight, the loveliest and most exciting experience of human life—but not either right or wrong in itself. It is rather regarded as a potent source of happiness or unhappiness, of morality or immorality. Everything depends on whether or not it can be controlled and directed along the lines of a social purpose, used to establish and strengthen the social institution of marriage.

The nineteenth century idolized and deified sexual love, and at the same time feared and dreaded it. The Victorian age was the age of Romance in which no praises were too fulsome or sickly sweet for the experience of physical passion. Yet when we now talk of Victorianism, what is uppermost in our minds? Prudery, Mrs. Grundy, and the suppression of frankness about sex. The romantic views about love were fanatically prevented from being brought to the test of fact. Now, that is the essence of sentimentality. It is emotional insincerity. And to this day, though with less and less effect among young people, romantic sentimentality has held the field. The real morality of the nineteenth century was the morality of principle, but it was poisoned by sentimentality so that it appeared as Social Utility. And we are suffering under the curse that it laid upon our fathers. Love was, in effect, made a stalking horse for social success, in all its multiform varieties; unconsciously, no doubt, but none the less effectively.

It worked like this. We kept young men and women in careful ignorance of the facts of sex. We instilled a sense of shame about them to this end and at the same time filled their minds with vague colourful ideas and emotions—romance. We kept a close guard over the meeting of boys and girls by a policy of segregation. When the time was ripe, we engineered a meeting of selected couples under conditions which would be likely to lead to a 'match', and made sure that nothing could come of it until they were safely married. Then with a sigh of relief we sent them off on a 'honeymoon' to discover the real facts for themselves. I do not believe that history can show an example of more barbarous duplicity and trickery than this. We are still too close to it to feel the grossness and vulgarity of deceit of which it is constituted. To talk of that sentimentality as a belief in love as the basis of morality is nonsense.

I have spent too long in sketching a background. Let me come straight away now to the one really positive thing I have to say about sex-morality. Its true basis is the virtue of chastity. And I want to explain what I think chastity really is. That I can make it very exact and clear I am not sure; but perhaps I can put you on the track of something that is absolutely vital. In a word, then, chastity is emotional sincerity.

We know pretty well what we mean by honesty, or *intellectual* sincerity. You will remember that I insisted earlier that the moral standard of Europe was an intellectual one. On the intellectual side our moral development has made us very sensitive to the intellectual virtues—the virtues of the mind. Telling the truth—the honesty of the mind—is I think the virtue to which we are most sensitive. We hate and despise the liar, and we recognize his duplicity easily. We feel in our bones that lying is shameful, despicable and immoral. What, then, is lying? It is expressing what you do not think, pretending to believe what you do not believe. That is what I mean by intellectual insincerity, the dishonesty of the mind. By emotional insincerity I mean the parallel of this in the emotional life. We are emotionally insincere when we express a feeling that we do not feel. If honesty is expressing what you think, chastity is expressing what you feel.

Let us go into the parallel a little more closely. Negative untruthfulness is simply expressing what you do not think; that is lying. But sincerity in the mind is much more than this. It is positively expressing what you do think and believe. To refrain from expressing what you think or believe or know to someone, if it is to his advantage or to someone else's advantage that he should know it, is positive dishonesty. We call it dissimulation—the suppression of the truth. In the same way, there is a positive and a negative insincerity of the emotions. The negative insincerity is to express a feeling that you do not feel. The positive is to fail to express what you do feel when it makes a real difference to the person from whom you conceal it. It is, then, a failure in chastity to express a feeling to someone that you do not feel;

to express love for a person, for instance, when you do not feel it. It is equally unchaste to conceal your feelings from someone to whom it makes a real difference.

Now, of course, it is difficult to be sincere—much more difficult than we usually imagine. But the point I wish to draw your attention to is this: that though we are sensitive to the moral need for intellectual sincerity, we are very insensitive to the need for emotional sincerity. We may excuse mental insincerity under certain circumstances, but we never, I think, would praise it as a virtue. Yet we constantly inculcate emotional insincerity as a duty, and praise people for concealing their real feelings, or pretending to feelings that they do not possess. We pretend to like the things that we are told we ought to like; we pretend that we feel sympathy for a person in distress, when we do not, and we not only see no harm in this, but we positively encourage it as a social virtue. In reality emotional sincerity is far more important than the sincerity of the mind, because it lies nearer to the heart of life and conduct. It is vicious to pretend about our feelings. It is something of which we ought to feel ashamed.

One other point we must notice. We know that a man who habitually trifles with the truth tends to lose the capacity to distinguish between truth and falsehood. It is dangerously easy to deceive ourselves about what we believe. If we keep repeating a story that is not true we come to believe in its truth ourselves. Now this holds good with even greater force in the emotional life. If we habitually cheat others about our feelings, we soon become unable to know what we really feel. If we act as though we love a person when we do not, we will come to believe that we do love him. If there is any truth about life that experience and modern psychology have together driven home to me it is this—that any pretence about our feelings results in self-deception. We become incapable of knowing what we really feel. I have heard Christian moralists say that the way to learn to love people whom you dislike is to behave to them as if you loved them. This, I am certain, is completely and dangerously false. Emotional pretence leads to emotional insensibility. If you express systematically to anyone, in word or action, a love which you do not feel, you will undoubtedly come to believe that you love him. But you will hate him without knowing it. That is what the psycho-analyst discovers. To tamper with the sincerity of your emotional life is to destroy your inner integrity, to become unreal for yourself and others, to lose the capacity of knowing what you feel. There is nothing more destructive of all that is valuable in human life. I am certain of this; not on theoretical grounds but because I discovered it in my own experience.

Now let us go a step further. What is called
Christian morality to-day is based upon a Stoic tradition; upon intellect and will, upon the suppression
of the emotional basis of conduct in the interest of
'principles'. The result of that is inevitable. Though
Europe has developed itself intellectually with a
steady growth upwards, has progressed in its grasp
of principle, in scholarship and understanding, in
the organization and control of life and of the world,
it has remained all but completely barbarous on the
emotional side. Our civilization, for all its scientific
and administrative capacity, has remained emotionally vulgar and primitive, unchaste in the extreme.
We do not recognize this, of course, because it is
simply the reflection of our own inner insensibility.
That insensibility is the inevitable result of a morality
based upon will and reason, imposing itself upon the
emotions and so destroying their integrity. Until we
insist upon emotional sincerity, until we cease playing
ducks and drakes with our feelings in the mistaken
desire to dragoon them into conformity with what
we conceive to be our 'duties', until we begin to trust
our emotional life, this state of affairs will necessarily
go on. Our sex-morality, in particular, will remain
blind, barbarous and unreal, a vulgarity and a
scandal.

Chastity, then, is emotional sincerity—sincerity in
the expression of what we feel; and it is the funda-

mental virtue, from one point of view, of a Christian morality. It is the emotional guide to good conduct, the proper determinant of personal relations. It is the condition of personal integrity. I am obviously using the word 'chastity' in a wider sense than is usual. I think myself that this is the proper use of the word— that it explains what an artist means when he says that a picture is chaste—that there is no striving after effect, and so no vamping of emotion; that it explains what Jesus meant when he said 'Blessed are the pure in heart for they shall see God'. I can think of no other word which will express what I feel about the majority of cinema films and of modern novels. They are unchaste; they arouse feelings that one doesn't really feel, by pretending emotions that the author doesn't feel. The use of the term in reference to sex is merely a special case, I think, like the similar restriction of the term 'morality' to mean sexual morality. But we shall not argue about words, especially as our main theme is the application of this guiding rule of emotional sincerity to the relations of men and women.

Let us return to the new phenomenon of modern society, the disappearance of the differentiation of the social functions of the sexes. Women are demanding that they should be individuals in the same sense that men are, that they should be independent, granted the same free initiative that men have in the choice of a vocation; in a word, that their social functions and duties should not be determined by their sex. This is a demand that in social relationships and activities sex should not count as a determining factor. Is that a right demand? Undoubtedly. It is, firstly, just as much a consequence of the teaching of Christ as that slavery is wrong. 'In Christ Jesus there is neither male nor female . . . neither bond nor free.' The gospel cannot admit functional distinctions as a basis of moral distinctions. The morality of the relations between men and women has nothing to do with the differences of sex, which belong to the physical and the organic, not to the personal plane. The proper relations between human beings are personal relations, in which organic differences have no essential standing. Difference of sex is on the same level as differences of natural capacity. Therefore, men and women must meet and enter into relationships on the personal level—not as male and female, but as human beings, equally made in the image of God. They must determine their relations to one another for themselves, as human persons, and not allow organic differences to determine their relations for them. There is only one proper ground of relationship between any two human beings, and that is mutual friendship. Difference of sex may make the friendship easier or more difficult of achievement, but it cannot make any difference in principle.

Further, if difference of sex is made an essential difference in human relations, then men and women are treated as complementary to one another. Each, then, has meaning and significance only in terms of the other. Neither is a real individual. Now this is a denial of human personality. It destroys the possibility of true friendship between them. Complete individual integrity is the condition of personal relationship. Otherwise you inevitably subordinate persons to their function. Moral relations are dependent on the absolute value of the human being, as a free human spirit, not as a man or a woman. It was this, I imagine, that Paul was feeling after when he advised Christians not to marry if they could help it, because, 'the husband will care for the things of this world, how he may please his wife'. If the relation is an organic one that is inevitable. And when you begin to live to please people, you destroy emotional sincerity. Love is ruled out because chastity is ruled out. Inner integrity is impossible. This is the recurrent tragedy of so many marriages that start with fair promise. The husband and wife are specialized in different directions, and the further each develops in his or her own function the wider the gulf between them becomes. They come to depend upon one another, and so lose their integrity—the very basis of personal unity. Dependence and freedom are incompatible. Yet freedom is the basis of all moral conduct.

Let me put this in another way because I feel that it is all-important. A mutual sexual attraction is no proper basis for a human relationship between a man and a woman. It is an organic thing, not personal. What, then, is a proper basis? Love is, between any two persons. Love may or may not include sexual attraction. It may express itself in sexual desire. But sexual desire is not love. Desire is quite compatible with personal hatred, or contempt, or indifference, because it treats its object not as a person but as a means to its own satisfaction. That is the truth in the statement that doing what we want to do is not the same as doing what we ought to do.

But notice this—that mutual desire does not make things any better. It only means that each of two persons is treating the other as a means of self-satisfaction. A man and a woman may want one another passionately without either loving the other. This is true not merely of sexual desire but of all desires. A man and a woman may want one another for all sorts of reasons, not necessarily sexual, and make that mutual want the basis of marriage, without either loving the other. And, I insist, such mutual desire, whether sexual or not, is no basis of a human relationship between them. It is no basis of friendship. It is the desire to obtain possession of another person for the satisfaction of their own needs; to dare to assert the claim over another human being—'You are mine!' That is unchaste and immoral, a definite inroad upon the integrity of a fellow human being. And the fact that the desire and the claim are mutual does not make a pennyworth of difference. Mutual love is the only basis of a human relationship; and bargains and claims and promises are attempts to substitute something else; and they introduce falsity and unchastity into the relationship. No human being can have rights in another, and no human being can grant to another rights in himself or herself. That is one of the things of which I am deeply convinced.

Now take another point. There is only one safeguard against self-deception in the face of desire, and that is emotional sincerity, or chastity. No intellectual principle, no general rule of judgment is of any use. How can a man or woman know whether they love another person or merely want them? Only by the integrity of his or her emotional life. If they have habitually been insincere in the expression of their feelings, they will be unable to tell. They will think they love when they only want another person for themselves. What is usually known as 'being in love' is simply being in this condition. It blinds us to the reality of other people; leads us to pretend about their virtues, beauties, capacities, and so forth; deprives us of the power of honest feeling and wraps us in a fog of unreality. That is no condition for any human being to be in. If you love a person you love

him or her in their stark reality, and refuse to shut
your eyes to their defects and errors. For to do that
is to shut your eyes to their needs.

Chastity, or emotional sincerity, is an emotional
grasp of reality. 'Falling in love' and 'being in love'
are inventions of romantic sentimentality, the inevitable result of the deceit and pretence and suppression from which we suffer. Love cannot abide
deceit, or pretence or unreality. It rests only in the
reality of the loved one, demands the integrity of its
object, demands that the loved one should be himself, so that it may love him for himself.

This indicates the true basis for *any* intimate personal relationship and applies universally between
persons, whether they are of the same or of different
sexes. What then of the morality of sexual intercourse? It falls, in the first place, within the wider
morality of personal relationship of which we have
been speaking, and is governed by it. Any intimate
human relationship must be based upon love and
governed by that emotional sincerity which is the
essence of chastity. Real personal love is the basis in
the absence of which specifically sexual relations are
unchaste and immoral. This holds inside marriage
just as much as outside it. The fact of marriage cannot make chaste what is in itself unchaste. I would
hazard the guess, without much fear that I was
wrong, that there is as much sexual immorality

inside marriage as outside it. Morality does not rest on externals.

In the second place, between two human beings who love one another, the sexual relationship is one of the possible expressions of love, as it is one of the possible co-operations in love—more intimate, more fundamental, more fraught with consequences inner and outer, but essentially one of the expressions of love, not fundamentally different in principle from any others, as regards its use. It is neither something high and holy, something to venerate and be proud of, nor is it something low and contemptible, to be ashamed of. It is a simple ordinary organic function to be used like all the others, for the expression of personality in the service of love. This is very important. If you make it a thing apart, to be kept separate from the ordinary functions of life, to be mentioned only in whispers; if you exalt it romantically or debase it with feelings of contempt (and if you do the one you will find that you are doing the other at the same time; just as to set women on a pedestal is to assert their inferiority and so insult their humanity); if you single out sex in that way as something very special and wonderful and terrible, you merely exasperate it and make it uncontrollable. That is what our society has done. It has produced in us a chronic condition of quite unnatural exasperation. There is a vast organization in our civilization for the stimulation of sex—clothes, pictures, plays, books, advertisements and so on. They keep up in us a state of sexual hypersensitiveness, as a result of which we greatly overestimate the strength and violence of natural sexuality. And the most powerful stimulant of sex is the effort to suppress it. There is only one cure, to take it up, simply, frankly and naturally into the circle of our activities; and only chastity, the ordinary sincerity of the emotional life, can enable us to do so.

Sex, then, must fall within the life of personality, and be an expression of love. For unlike all our other organic functions it is essentially mutual. If it is to be chaste, therefore, it must fall within a real unity of two persons—within essential friendship. And it must be a necessary part of that unity. The ideal of chastity is a very high and difficult one, demanding an emotional unity between a man and a woman which transcends egoism and selfish desire. In such a unity sex ceases to be an appetite—a want to be satisfied—and becomes a means of communion, simple and natural. Mutual self-satisfaction is incompatible with chastity, which demands the expression of a personal unity already secured. Indeed, it seems to me, that it is only when such a unity in friendship has reached a point where it is shut up to that expression of itself that it is completely chaste. How can two people know that their love demands such an expression? Only through a mutual chastity, a complete emotional sincerity between them. That alone can be the touchstone of reality. Only that can save us from self-deception where strong feelings are engaged, and preserve our emotions unsullied by organic excitement, free for their personal function, to grasp the realities of value in persons and in the world outside us. That is the crux of personal relation always. In sex it is only more difficult to maintain. Sex-love, if it is love at all, is a personal communion in which a man and a woman meet in the full integrity of their personal reality. And the law of reality in the relationship of persons is this. 'The integrity of persons is inviolable. You shall not use a person for your own ends, or indeed for any ends, individual or social. To use another person is to violate his personality by making an object of him; and in violating the integrity of another you violate your own.' In all enjoyment there is a choice between enjoying the other and enjoying yourself through the instrumentality of the other. The first is the enjoyment of love, the second is the enjoyment of lust. When people enjoy themselves through each other, that is merely mutual lust. They do not meet as persons at all; their reality is lost. They meet as ghosts of themselves and their pleasure is a ghostly pleasure that cannot begin to satisfy a human soul, and which only vitiates its capacity for reality.

Does the distinction between enjoying yourself in your friends' company and enjoying your friends seem a too subtle philosopher's distinction? I assure you, from experience of friendship—not from study of logic —that the distinction is the root of the difference between morality and immorality, between love and lust. It is a distinction not to be argued, but to be felt; and chastity is the capacity to feel it and to live by it. For it is the distinction between reality and unreality in the emotional life, which controls the springs of conduct, and chastity is the sincerity of the emotions.

That is the positive thing I have to say. I have no doubt that it leaves you perplexed and puzzled. It seems to have no definite bearing upon practical problems. You want to ask me: 'Will it preserve the sanctity of marriage?' So far as marriage has a sanctity it will preserve it; so far as it has not it will destroy it. This may look like dodging the issue, but I cannot help it. If you ask me 'Will chastity prevent men and women from having sexual intercourse outside marriage?' I can only answer 'I don't know.' 'But that is surely the really important point,' you may urge. I answer: 'It is *not* the important point. Compared with the importance of personal reality, of chastity, it is a point of no significance.' There could only be one reason for wanting to answer it, the desire to substitute a social rule for spiritual chastity. We want to be able to approve and condemn other people by the externals of their conduct, and to approve and condemn ourselves by the conformity of our actions to a rule. To that Christ answers: 'Judge not, that ye be not judged.' You say, perhaps, that it is a very dangerous position; there is no security in it. Since when has the truth become the line of least resistance, an insurance against danger and insecurity and the need of faith and courage? The danger is merely the danger of life, and there is only one way of escape from that danger, and that is to die. There is a spiritual death; and it is possible to commit spiritual suicide from fear of the terrors of spiritual reality. That is the only *real* danger. If you wish for 'security' you can have it at the price of spiritual death. You can fence in your soul with bulwarks of rules and forms, trenches of prohibitions and exhortations, to protect it from the inroads of the armies of the spirit. You can refuse to traffic with men and women in the sterling gold of your own precious life. Like the man in the parable, you may wrap up your capital in a clean handkerchief and bury it, for fear of the risks of trading with it in a world where even banks go bankrupt. You may hope so to render it up at last and say: 'I have kept it safe; see how clean my soul is, unspotted from the earth.' And the judge will say: 'Take it from him, and cast him into outer darkness.

If you choose security you will have your reward: you may gain the whole world. You may escape all the dangers of reality. All but one! In the long run— and for those of us who are fortunate, it comes before the hour of death—a voice will say: 'Thou fool! This day thy soul shall be required of thee. Then whose will these things be? For what shall it profit a man if he shall gain the whole world and lose his own soul?'

ART AND THE FUTURE

THE THREE generalized expressions of the personal—science, art, and religion—can only be properly understood in relation to one another. Of the three, religion is the fully concrete expression; the other two are partial and abstract. To understand either art or science we must grasp the principle of abstraction through which they arise, and so recognize the form of their derivation from religion. We have to understand how science and art are unified and contained in principle in the religious expression. This understanding, in turn, is only possible if we start from the particular facts of common experience—the particular expressions of the personal—of which religion, art and science are the generalized forms.

The simplest clue to this interrelation of the three generalized expressions of the personal is to be found in the grammatical distinction of three persons. Language is primarily a means of communication between persons; and it is only natural that its fundamental forms should reflect the structure of personal experience. The immediate necessities of language in its primary function of inter-personal expression determine that the forms of our speech shall recognize a distinction between a first, a second and a third person; between the speaker, the listener, and the person or thing which is the object spoken about. This grammatical distinction between the 'I', the 'you', and the 'he, she or it', is clearly derived from what we might call the speech-situation. Now the capacity for rational speech is a defining characteristic of the personal, and therefore the speech-situation is a situation which contains the full defining form of the personal, provided that the occasion of speech which we consider is one in which the full nature of speech finds expression. Such an occasion is to be found in the conversation of friends, where speech is used as a means of mutual self-expression.

Conversation between two intimate friends is not merely an interchange of information, but also a means of fellowship. Through speech they enter into communion. This is the particular experience which is generalized in religion. When two friends talk together they talk about something or someone. It is impossible to dispense with the third person. There must be a subject of conversation. The giving and receiving of information is an essential element in all speech. It is the irreducible factor in every communication. But in the conversation of friends it is not the most significant element. I do not mean that they talk together for the sake of talking: when people do that they are not in fellowship, and the conversation is meaningless. They are both interested in what they are talking about, and intent upon it. But what gives to the conversation its personal significance is the mutual sharing of experience and knowledge. They do not merely give away information; they give themselves away to one another. This is so much the core of the experience that the things talked about may be quite trivial things; yet their triviality does not lessen the significance of the occasion, nor does it result in boredom. For in such communication the third person derives its significance from the relationship of the two persons who talk about it together. It need not have any significance in itself apart from the significance that their fellowship lends it. If we are friends and in touch with one another, what we talk about and what we say about it becomes a bridge across the gulf that separates our individualities; a bridge for the mutual commerce of personality over which our separate selves can pass to meet and enter into unity. This may seem mysterious in statement, and difficult for our understanding; but it is a commonplace of our everyday experience.

I should like to draw attention in passing to a formal characteristic of this full speech-situation, which is of great importance for its comprehension, though it does not directly concern our immediate purpose. It would be wrong to say of it that the third person—the object spoken about—is merely a *means* to the mutual self-expression of two friends. The category of means and end is here out of place. The object is the mutual focus of interest, and it is a condition of their fellowship that it should be. They do not speak about it with the purpose of revealing themselves to one another. On the contrary, it is because they are in touch with one another that they find their interest in the object aroused and sustained. Their friendship makes the things they talk about a common focus of interest. It is not related to their fellowship as means to an end. If it were, they would be talking for talking's sake, and neither would be really interested in what was said. An element of dishonesty would enter into their relation which would frustrate the purpose. We know well enough that people can converse together to conceal their fear or shyness of one another, to deceive one another as to their real intentions, or because there they are and they must kill time. They may talk to impress one another by their wit or their intelligence. In such cases speech is used as a means to an end. But these are dishonesties of conversation, and not the free communication of persons in satisfactory relation with one another. The conversation of friends stands in strong contrast with these. It is not a means to an end, but something wider and more inclusive. Neither is it an end in itself. It is a way of being together in personal communion. It is the temporal and changing expression of an eternal and unchanging unity between them. It is what it is and has the significance it has because it springs from, is sustained by and contained in the mutuality of their personal relationship. It is this mutual self-communication in speech that forms the simplest full experience of the personal. The generalized expression of it is religion.

Now let us consider how science and art can be derived from this full speech-situation. Suppose that the same conversation takes place between two strangers who have no personal interest in one another. There is then no self-communication involved. The object has to provide in itself the whole of the common interest. Each separately is interested in the thing discussed for its own sake, and not at all for the sake of the other person's interest in it, so that the total significance of the speech-situation resides, for the persons concerned, in the object. Thus the object, the third person, becomes the essence of the situation, and the conversation becomes a matter of giving and receiving information about it. The full speech-situation has been degraded to an impersonal level, and at that level the experience is no longer emotional, but merely intellectual; no longer religious but scientific, for it is of this type of experience that science is the generalized form.

Science, in the full sense, is the systematic development to universality of this information-giving and information-receiving attitude in personal relations. It is therefore profoundly impersonal. It seeks to degrade language from its primary use as a means of self-communication, by eradicating from it all the character, the complex of imagery and magic, which makes it a carrier of emotion and a means of self-communication. For science is only interested in the object, and therefore writes, speaks and thinks, even of itself, in the third person; like a child that has not yet become self-conscious. There is no 'I' nor 'you' for science, only 'it'; and because of this science is utterly at sea in the personal field. As soon as the scientist is disturbed by a strong emotion, his work is deranged; he ceases to be scientific and becomes a human being. When he escapes from the real world of home and friendship and the traffic of life, and shuts himself into his laboratory, he escapes from himself and loses himself in a world of information.

Of information, however, not of knowledge. Knowledge is always personal, always somebody's; but information is just anybody's. Science wants facts, atoms of information, which must all be indifferent to their being known; all equally valid for anybody at all. Science is not the personal knowledge of this scientist or of that; it is information, the raw material out of which you and I can pick and choose what we want for our purposes, to build up our own knowledge, which is real knowledge just because it is ours and nobody else's.

Because science is impersonal it is always worried about the 'observer'. It wants to find an 'absolute observer', an indifferent observer, that is to say an impersonal observer, a person who isn't a person. For only a person can even hold information, while no person can *merely* hold it. Whoever he is, he is sure to do something with it that makes it a little more than information, perhaps by using it to make a corner in wheat, perhaps merely by getting excited about it and colouring it with his emotion, perhaps by using it to show his wife what an admirable fellow he is.

This concentration on the object, this indifference to the persons concerned, which is characteristic of the 'information' attitude, is often called objectivity. It is really only impersonality. For the strange thing is that when we concentrate on the 'object'—the third person, what we talk about—to the exclusion of the persons who know it and talk about it, we lose the reality of the object. Information is always information about something, not knowledge of it. Science cannot teach you to know your dog; it can only tell you about dogs in general. You can only get to know your dog by nursing him through distemper, teaching him how to behave about the house, and playing ball with him. Of course you can *use* the information that science gives you about dogs in general to get to know your dog better, but that is another matter. Science is concerned with generalities, with more or less universal characteristics of things in general, not with anything in particular. And anything real is always something in particular. In some queer way things depend for the knowledge of them upon our personal interest in them. So soon as we depersonalize our attitude to them, they withhold their secret and dissolve away into sets of general characteristics floating in an ether of abstract intellect. Science (and philosophy too, though to a lesser extent) is always baffled by reality; the very nature of their approach destroys it by dissolving it away. The concentration upon the object, so far from facilitating knowledge of the object, makes it impossible; precisely because it disregards the personal relation in which alone knowledge is possible. They have their reward: in losing their souls philosophy and science gain the whole world—of information.

This talk of science is only by way of a background to the understanding of the place of art in the personal world. Art, too, can be simply derived from the full personal experience which we are considering. If science wipes out the first and second persons and

the personal relation between them by reducing
them to the status of bearers of information, art too
makes its own abstraction. It abstracts from, and so
universalizes the second person. I should try to put
this concretely and pictorially. We start again with
our two friends in real conversation. We shall suppose
that they have just met after the Christmas vacation
and are sharing with one another the pleasure of
their holiday. One has been for the first time to
Switzerland for winter sports. He begins to tell his
friend of the glory of sunset in winter in the Bernese
Oberland, with the creamy pink light flooding the
immense quiet snow-spaces and the crumpled
glaciers; picking out the dark rugged line of long
mountain ridge against the fathomless tenderness of
the sky. 'How sharp the silver spear-heads charge,
Where Alp meets heaven in snow!' This is no scientific description; dispensed, labelled and docketed
information; but information clothed in the flesh of
imagery and pulsing with the blood of emotion—a
communication of self. Now imagine that in the
telling he becomes so wrapped and thrilled in his
experience that he becomes indifferent to the personality of his listener; that the friend becomes just
somebody—anybody—to whom he can express himself about the marvel of that night at Mürren; then
he has become the artist and his talk is the essence of
art. He must communicate himself by telling what

he saw; for that he must have a listener; it is a listener he needs, and anyone will do, provided he will listen, really listen and enjoy. The artist wants to give, not to receive; so that mutuality is lost, and his experience, though it remains intensely personal, is one-sided, has lost part of the fullness of personal experience. Knowledge there is, and the pouring out of knowledge, which is self-expression, but not mutuality; and therefore the second person is generalized to a listener, negative and receptive, and tends to fade out of the picture and become hypothetical and imaginary. The artist can write his description for anyone to read, or paint his picture for anyone to see. He gives himself, not to anyone in particular, but to the world at large. That is not a fuller but a narrower experience; because personally, to give yourself to everyone, is to give yourself to no one. The mutuality of the personal belongs to its essence.

Art, then, like science, is an abstraction from the full unity and wholeness of the personal. Yet it remains personal in a sense that science is not; and its value is higher than the value of science, because its abstractedness is lower. Science universalizes and so neglects both the first and the second persons. Art generalizes only the second. In this art gains two advantages over science. By retaining the object in full relation to the artist—the first person—art secures knowledge of the object by maintaining its reality; and also it secures, for the same reason, the free creativeness of the person. These two achievements are the essence of art—its two aspects of receptivity and spontaneity, and they deserve a little further consideration.

The receptivity of art, the artistic consciousness of the object, is *knowledge proper*, as distinct from the understanding of or information about the object, which is all that science can give us. The artistic attitude alone enables us to come into contact with the reality of things, to realize the individuality, the value of actual objects, actual people. For science things exist only in terms of something else. Reality is that which exists in and for itself, the individual. Knowledge is the grasp of reality, the contemplation of the individual in its own proper being. This is precisely what art gives us and science does not; therefore the receptivity of art is knowledge; the receptivity of science is not. For the same reason the value of science is utility-value, while the value of art is intrinsic. Why is this? It is because science remains subjective, while art achieves objectivity. Any real object is for science only an example, a fact, something to be referred to a class, something to be analysed into elements (the more unsubstantial the better), something which is the effect of something else. Thus science is endlessly referred from one thing to another and chases objectivity over the infinite cosmos, finding, like Noah's dove, no place on which the sole of its foot may rest. For science reality is always round the next corner. But art never has to seek objectivity, because it is objective from the beginning. It rests in the object of its choice, stirring only to penetrate deeper into the heart of its reality. It enjoys its object, and without such an interest in the object for its own sake, it is impossible to grasp any reality at all. Science cannot rest in any object, just because it is not interested in any; its interest is subjective, in the operations of the mind upon the object, in doing something to it, describing it, referring it, never in the object itself, in and for itself, in its individual reality. The receptivity of art, the attitude of contemplation, is our only source of the knowledge of reality. Ultimately it is the condition of science itself.

The spontaneity of art, on the other hand, is personal creativeness, or self-expression. There is a modern dispute in the philosophy of æsthetics which is concerned to determine whether art is intuition or expression. It is in fact, as we can now see, both at once—intuition as the receptivity by which we contemplate reality; expression as the spontaneity by which we express it for ourselves and so express ourselves through it. Knowledge is a mere receptivity and, therefore, negative, in itself nothing. It can exist only within a spontaneity, as an aspect of creative activity. Knowledge, even in the lowest sense, as scientific information, can only exist at all by virtue of an expression of it; and if the knowledge is real knowledge, that is to say, personal knowledge, it can only be maintained or realized by a personal expression. The artist, therefore, requires, even for the knowledge of reality, the creative spontaneity through which he expresses himself.

Creative spontaneity, the quality which the real artists show us in abstraction from what normally conceals it, is the essence of personal individuality. I must stress that point. All of us, without exception, because we are persons, are essentially artists. The capacity for creative self-expression is our birthright; it is what makes us human. Genius is no mysterious gift that some magical power confers on one man in a million. It is not something unique and supernatural. It is simply human spontaneity, the expression of personal freedom. That this seems a startling paradox is simply a measure of the derangement of our inner life, of our failure to be our human selves. The artist is not abnormal, but simply the normal human individual. Not of course the *average* human being, after education and the constraints of social and physical necessity have succeeded in suppressing and stunting his natural capacity. The normal, when we are dealing with spontaneity, is always and necessarily ideal, since only the ideal can be a standard for persons. Remove the restrictions, both inner and outer, which suppress the spontaneity of any human being, and his natural spontaneity will show itself as artistic creativeness. If we are not in effective possession of this capacity, we are not ourselves; there is something the matter somewhere, though the blame may not be ours. In fact, the great hindrance to art is fear and its outward manifestation, the demand for security. We are afraid of ourselves, and so afraid to be ourselves. We are afraid of the spontaneity of others, therefore we build up, individually and socially, a great network of defences against the desperate spontaneity and creativeness of the personal. Primarily each of us is afraid of himself; because of this we are afraid of others; and these secret fears in the mass are the root of the injustice and squalor of our civilization. The supreme condemnation of a civilization is that it is inartistic, that is to say, impersonal, inhuman, unreal. The absence of art is the absence of spontaneity, of proper humanity; the penalty for it is an inner stultification, a loss of spiritual integrity, a slowing down of the pulses of the inner life. We become ghosts to ourselves and to others. A civilization that has lost the capacity of the artist is a prey to spiritual paralysis, to an inner rotting of its human powers. The best that can be hoped for is that the repressed spontaneity should rebel, even if the rebellion is a manifestation of destructive rather than creative spontaneity; even if it has to make a clean sweep of the forms and institutions that are stifling it, and start rebuilding a human life from the beginning. If we are to make peace in the world, we must make peace with our own souls.

One point in particular we should notice about the spontaneity of art. It is essentially self-expression. But self-expression is only possible through the object. This is due to the objectivity of the personal. Our personality *is* our objectivity. Our reality is a going out of ourselves to a reality beyond us and independent of us. Shut me up within the limits of my own organism, rob me of my capacity to pass beyond the limitations of my subjectivity, to enter into and enjoy that which is not me—then I become a mere animal, conscious not of things but merely of the excitements and images which they stimulate in me. The self is personal; and the expression of the self is personal. Self-expression is the expression of that capacity to enter into the life of the other and to be absorbed in it. It is because the artist loses himself in the reality of that which he describes or depicts or reveals, because of his individual self-effacement, that his work is a spontaneous expression of himself. That is one meaning of the penetrating saying of Jesus: 'He that saveth his life shall lose it, and he that loseth his life shall keep it unto life eternal.' Personal spontaneity is always objective, always in terms of the independent reality of an object which absorbs us. There is no other self-expression possible. If we block the avenues of the outpouring of self, if we withdraw from the reality of the world, if we allow our actions to be subjectively determined by mere instincts and habits, following our inclinations, we do not express ourselves, we frustrate our own self-expression, surrender our freedom and suffocate all creative spontaneity. The artist does not act by impulse, still less by the compulsion of rules, but by the nature of the reality which he apprehends. By doing this he becomes free and his action becomes a self-expression. In no other way can self-expression be achieved. In particular it cannot be achieved by will or purpose. The man of iron will is always the man who cannot be spontaneous, who cannot act in terms of reality, who cannot be free.

Thus, art is essentially the spontaneity of persons expressing themselves through the reality of the object. It would be natural at this point to go on to consider the nature of artistic creativeness. But we must postpone this for a moment in order to consider the limitations of art which arise through the absence of mutuality, the generalizing of the second person. If the second person has become simply anybody who cares to read my poem, there is no need for the give and take which mutual conversation demands. I can take time to contemplate my subject; I can draft and redraft my expression of it, make it complete and whole in itself, a rounded, finished work, which can stand by itself. For instance, a modern artist told me some time ago how he painted a portrait of one of the old Pharaohs of Egypt. It involved the study of all existing statues and representations of him. It involved months of patient research in the library of the British Museum about the times in which he lived, the social order and religious beliefs in which he was nursed, making use of all that science has unearthed in the way of information about him and his fellows. (For art includes and uses science, and it is the master for whom science toils.) And it involved the mastery of the reality beneath such information, and laborious effort to give expression to it in the portrait. Obviously all this would be impossible in the reciprocity of mutual life. The second person must be removed to a distance and forgotten. But these gains, which make art as a separate pursuit (as distinguished from art as an element in the personal life), a possibility at all, are counterbalanced by a serious loss, and from the elimination of the second person the limitations of art and its ideal arise. Two of these limitations we may note and consider—the fragmentariness of art and the unreality of its creations.

In the first place, art, like science, is fragmentary. Science is only real as a collection of separate sciences, each with its own department of investigation and its own limitations. It is a condition of the existence of science that it should be fragmentary in this sense. Philosophy, on the other hand, is one; there are not many philosophies in the sense that there are many sciences, however many varieties of philosophical theory there may be. Similarly, art can only exist as a collection of separate arts—music, painting, architecture, dancing and so on. Art must so limit itself; there cannot be an art-in-general. Religion, on the contrary, like philosophy, which is its parallel, is one, and there cannot be separate religions in the sense that there are separate arts. Philosophy and religion deal with the whole in its wholeness and unity: science and art are fragmentary and deal with fragments of reality.

This fragmentariness of art goes much deeper than the mere distinction of the various arts, which is based ultimately on the distinction of the various senses through which we can apprehend the world. That fragmentariness, like the fragmentariness of science, is concerned with the third person, the object. More important is the fragmentariness that results from the isolation of the self (the first person) from the mutuality of personal intercourse. Art can provide no basis for co-operation. Each artist is confined within the limits of his own acquaintance with the world, within his individual objectivity. No artist can speak for art, only for himself as an isolated artist. Only the individuality of the personal can be expressed by art; and since the experience of the individual is but a fragment of personal experience, his art can only express a fragment of the personal. Of that fragment he has to make a complete self-sufficient unity, since he deals with reality, and reality is individual. Thus we cannot add the revelation of one artist to the revelation of another to make up a whole revelation of reality. Artists are not complementary to each other: their work is essentially individual and exclusive. They are just different, and there is no bond of unity between their different visions. This is the first inevitable consequence of abstracting from the second person and losing mutuality.

But because of the vital relation between the artist and the object, between the first and third persons in art, this isolation of the artist and the fragmentariness of his vision of reality is reflected back into his actual work. The work of each artist is a collection of separate works, each of which is self-contained and exclusive of all the others. They have no unity among themselves. Each, of course, is a self-expression of the same person and, therefore, they possess a unity in relation to him. Thus all attempts to deal with the work of a single artist as a unity are driven to seek the clue to the system of them not in the works themselves but in the artist, in terms of his personal experience, his philosophy of life, his personal interests. In themselves the works are just different, each complete within its own boundaries, each failing, in so far as it needs any reference beyond itself. This is the main reason for the assertion that art is not bound by morality, that it is not concerned with assessing right and wrong, that a novelist's characters may all be vicious or feeble, that a painter's subject may be morally degrading, without any detriment to the artistic value that it possesses. This is in a sense true, but it is the result of the essential limitation of art, its fragmentariness. Good and evil are personal in the full sense, without abstraction; morality is concerned not merely with fragments of reality, with real individuals in isolation, but also with the inter-relation of reals, with reality as a whole. The artist is not the full human being, just because of the abstraction which isolates him. The mere artist would be necessarily amoral for lack of mutuality and would therefore fail of the fullness of the personal. The mere scientist would be something lower still. He would suffer not merely from amorality but also from anæsthesia. So Darwin lamented in his old age that his mind had become a mere machine for grinding out general laws, and wished that he had read a poem a day. And the artist notoriously tends to treat other persons as objects, and so to fail in the fullness of moral relationships.

Now, let us turn in conclusion to the second great limitation of art, the unreality of its creations. I gave this lecture the title of 'Art and the Future' in view of this final stage of the discussion, because it enables us to envisage the true place of art in a personal society in the Kingdom of the Future, which is the Kingdom of God. Art, as the spontaneity of the personal, is the great creative force of the world of persons. The artist is creator; he isolates himself, stands on the reality of his own experience in order to give himself to the world, not to this person or to that, but to anyone who will accept his gift. And yet he cannot wholly give himself, because of his isolation. He cannot give his receptivity; he cannot give his co-operation. As artist he is all spontaneity, and cannot take as well as give. The full life of the personal is a continual give and take. For that very reason he is completely dependent upon the takers, and must await their pleasure. That is why the artist, in a peculiarly desperate fashion, is always at the mercy of society.

To give oneself is to create. But to give oneself to people in general is to create something in general, and reality is always something in particular. The thing-in-general is always in the broad sense an idea; that quasi-reality whose existence is a reference beyond itself. The artist cannot, therefore, create reality but only a vision of reality, an image, a form, an idea in a sense like that which Plato grasped and took for reality itself. A work of art is always in this sense an idea, the form of something, nothing actual. This is, I think, our experience of works of art. They express to us some actual phase or aspect or fragment of the real, and they reveal an intimacy of knowledge of the real that all our science and philosophy can never show. But that is not all; in expressing this with a profound insight they create something, something that is not actual but which moves us to desire it. What is it that the artist creates? Beauty, people say. Perhaps; but beauty is a mere word, and answers no question. I suggest that he creates the possibility of a reality that is not yet, the idea of a future reality more perfect than the actual world we know. The artist is the architect of the real future; the architect but not the builder. And he is an architect who cannot hire builders to execute his plan. He must persuade them, wielding an authority, as Rousseau finely said, which is no authority. Nor can he stoop to cajolery and the trick of persuasion; for if he does, there can be no building. The plans the artist draws for the construction of reality are bound by the laws of reality just as much as those of the architect are bound by the laws of stress and strain, and by the materials to his hand. He must persuade by the power of his own knowledge of the actual real. So he must take his chance of finding listeners who will accept his proposals, listeners who are convinced by the reality of his vision. That will depend upon their own knowledge of reality, upon their artistic receptivity. If there are none such to listen he will be a voice crying in the wilderness, a despairing voice that cries: 'Ye will not come unto me, that ye might have life.'

Science cannot create the future for us. It can only provide the means and the materials. It is a complete and disastrous mistake to imagine that if science provides the materials, the general business of social evolution will see to the construction. The organic evolves; the personal is created, and created by persons. The spontaneity of the personal, which is art, is the capacity we possess to create reality. That capacity depends upon the knowledge of actual reality: not the information about it that science gives, but the grasp of it that the artist possesses. But the artist in isolation cannot create more than the vision of what may be, the possibility of the future. For the full creation of the future reality the receptivity which recognizes and thrills to the artist's vision is essential. In sober language, if this country is to have a future, if we are to create a society even a little better than the ramshackle patchwork which we live in at the moment, we shall have to attend to the artists, and learn how to attend. And it is the modern artists that we must look to in our need; the old masters are useless. They have no knowledge of the actual world in which we live, out of which a new world might be created. The craze for what is old and what has stood the appraisal of the centuries is a symptom of the fear of art rather than of the love of it. The cult of the antique may develop taste, but it tends to destroy artistic receptivity. For the old has done its work of social transformation. It remains as a monument of beauty. But a living work of art strikes always at the roots of our complacency and its beauty is hidden by its attack upon our security and our traditions.

There are three cultures upon which the modern world is built—the Hebrew, the Greek and the Roman—a religious, an æsthetic and a scientific culture. All of them, however, were unselfconscious; and in coming to consciousness they destroyed themselves. Modern civilization—already it is a little absurd to call it European—is based upon self-consciousness. It has been until now running through its first phase—the scientific phase. Its second phase must be an artistic one, and it is to this that we must now look forward. There has never yet been a true artistic culture in the world. There have been sporadic anticipations of the age of art which is still to come, and the first stirrings of which we can feel among us now. Almost the only great thinker who understood the possibilities of art was Plato—and in terror of its spontaneity and creativeness he banished it from his ideal Republic. The later world, less ruthless because less understanding, has sought to sidetrack the spontaneity of art, to use the artist as the decorator of a civilization whose real business lies elsewhere. But art is no adornment of life, no amusement or relaxation for energies that are weary of the serious work of civilization, no 'purgation of pity and fear', no safety-valve for an excess of emotion, no laboratory for the sublimation of dangerous passions. It is the spontaneity of the personal, the expression of self, the creation of the vision of what might be real, and therefore the architect of the future. We have to build the future. But it is mere insanity to build without an architect—even with a completed science to fetch and carry for us.

SCIENCE AND RELIGION

For centuries, until relatively recent times, the pride and prejudice of religion tyrannized over the minds and consciences and even the bodies of men. The one nation in history which was religious by nature—the Hebrews—came to self-consciousness in Jesus and so destroyed its own nationalism, just as the Greeks, the one naturally artistic nation, came to self-consciousness in Plato and rejected art, destroying its own æsthetic naturalism. The tradition of Jesus flowed into the vast organization of the Roman civilization, got mixed up with Stoicism and perverted by its fight with pagan worships, and ultimately triumphed by compromise. With the break-up of the Roman empire, the Church fell heir to the Roman spirit and the Roman authority and transformed the Roman Empire into a religious imperialism that aimed at and largely achieved a universal dominion over the spirit of civilized humanity. This religious imperialism, under the pseudonym of Christianity, gathered to itself and subjected to its purpose all the powers of the human spirit and made itself the arbiter of truth in theology, philosophy and science, of beauty in art, of social and individual right in morals, manners and politics, until it had blotted personal freedom from the earth, or bound it in chains. But there are limits to the possible suppression of the spontaneity of the human spirit, however mighty are the forces which an aristocracy of pride can enlist in support of its tyranny. The rediscovery of the art of Greece awakened the mediæval spirit to the artistic spontaneity of the Renaissance, which in turn led to the rediscovery of the religious spontaneity of Jesus in the Reformation. From that moment the vast tissue of prejudice which was called Christianity was doomed. The process of its disintegration was gradual, and is not even yet complete—though nearing its completion. For in the spheres of religion and art the Reformation was a negative and destructive movement; the continuous disruption of Protestantism into sectarian fragments which enfeebled themselves by their struggle with one another for universal authority is the major effect of its historical development. The one creative achievement of the Reformation was science and the scientific spirit. Science is thus the legitimate child of a great religious movement, and its genealogy goes back to Jesus. In its true sense, science is the one proper, positive expression of Christianity that the world has yet seen. The rest of modern culture—its

172

art, morality, and religion—is simply the disrupted remnants of the pseudo-Christianity of the mediæval world. That is why the newly awakened pagan world clutches at our science while scorning our culture, though the awakening itself is largely the effect of Christian missions with their destructive power over sham faiths.

The disruptive force of the Protestant Reformation tore the religion which lies at the basis of our culture into two competing parts, competing, both of them, for the establishment of the old autocracy. Its authoritative control of the inner springs of human life was the nut over which they wrangled and disputed; while science, the child to which the Reformation had given birth, grew up without much care or attention—so intent were the rivals on their struggle. Under such circumstances filial piety was naturally discouraged; and when science, come of age, entered upon the stage as arbiter of the dispute, it was only to crack the nut, give either party half of the shell and keep the kernel for himself.

During the earlier stages of its development, science had to struggle for its very existence against religious prejudice. A religious system whose pride forced it to claim supreme authority in all matters of belief, to fix the goal of philosophy and the conclusions of science in advance of the evidence, inevitably sought to exterminate all beliefs which tended to undermine its own authority. For a long time it succeeded in limiting the influence of science upon the minds and institutions of men. But in spite of jealousy and superstition and the fear they breed, science triumphed. The turning-point was the great controversy over evolution. That battle won—and it was won to all intents and purposes by the end of the nineteenth century—science was supreme, and religion steadily lost ground, influence and power, till in our own day religion, if still existent, is impotent.

But it is difficult to fight an enemy who uses such underground methods without learning to use them oneself. And in the hour of its triumph science has become as full of pride and prejudice as ever religion was. Its prejudice against religion is perhaps natural when we remember history, but it is neither wise nor chivalrous to a beaten enemy. Its pride in its achievements is perhaps more justifiable by comparison, though in themselves they are both very limited and also the work essentially of a rather small band of great men. But the pride of science in what it hasn't done and proposes to do in the future is much less reasonable and often quite ridiculous. There is nothing like pride for blinding us to our own limitations, driving us to assert as truth what is only our own speculative opinion, and stirring us up to make extravagant claims for our own capacities.

Modern science is very liable to superstition, and

174

tends to breed superstition in its devotees. The visionary dream of the mediæval church of a universal empire over the hearts of mankind, purified by obedience and submission, was not so madly irrational as the modern dream of a world made peaceful and happy by obedience to the dictates of scientific thought. The formula of the three persons in one God is sensible and significant when you put it side by side with the meaninglessness of the fundamental formula of scientific faith, that one and one makes two. The belief in the ether—which is still alive in science, though rather sick and bedridden—is as much a 'credo quia impossibile' as ever Tertullian's faith was; and scientists as well as priests are well versed in the practice of saying their Articles with mental reservations, or in pretending that they haven't changed their minds when they obviously have. We have heard it said that science will put an end to war by making it so horrible that for very fear nations will restrain their passions. Similarly the mediæval church tried to make hell so terrible that men would be frightened into curbing their evil desires. To me at least the scientists' terrorism seems the more gruesome, for war is at least something real, no figment of the imagination. When Galileo made two unequal weights reach the ground together after dropping them from the top of the leaning tower of Pisa, it was obvious to most mediævals that he was in league with the devil. And when a young man nowadays gets worried and melancholy about his sins it is equally obvious to the majority of scientists that something has gone wrong with his endocrine secretions. I don't know which of these two obviousnesses is the grosser superstition. There are fashions in superstition as there are in hats, and the current superstitions are scientific. There is even a superstition called Christian Science. Pride and prejudice are the parents of superstition; and superstition is the deadliest enemy of truth. But superstition is not religion because it masquerades in the cloak of religion; neither is it science because it masks itself in scientific terminology.

At the moment there is much talk about a struggle between science and religion, and of reconciliations between them. Terms of peace are drawn up from week to week, none of which have so far been accepted and signed. The interesting point about this is that it signifies a new strengthening of religion and a weakening of science. It is not unconnected with the remarkable development of art in recent years, and of popular interest in art. For art is in certain important respects the natural ally of religion; and it is much more definitely anti-scientific, at least in our own day. It is not for nothing that Mr. Middleton Murry writes on God, and that Mr. Aldous Huxley's attack on science in a novel is so shrewd that it calls forth an apologetic in the columns of *Nature*; nor that D. H. Lawrence, the most consummate artist of them all, spent half his energy in an attack upon the intellect and all its works. These are signs of the times. And religion is taking heart again, while science seems a little disturbed and a little humbler. Such a situation is conducive to a *rapprochement*, and peace-feelers are put out from one side and from the other. Why, otherwise, should we be discussing the question ourselves?

But why all this pother, it is said, about science and religion? There can be no quarrel between them: each has its place in life and they cannot ultimately be in contradiction. Theoretically, perhaps, and formally, this is correct. It is not difficult to philosophize about the matter in one's study, and to assign each its place in a scheme of the perfect life. Indeed, I feel sure that it could be done easily in a dozen different (and contradictory) ways, each of which would seem satisfactory—and be as useless in practice as shooting at a tiger with a pop-gun. Science and religion are not logical definitions. They are forces in the world of men, and in the minds of men. The struggle between science and religion goes on in us, and it is a real struggle, a dramatic struggle, often a tragic struggle. It is not a controversy between science in the abstract and religion in the abstract; not even between religious people and scientific people, between whom a *modus vivendi* could be found on a basis of live-and-let-live. It is a deep-seated schism in the personal life of every intelligent modern man who wishes to be honest and sincere with himself. Can I be at once sincerely scientific and sincerely religious? Is the scientific temper in me compatible with my tendencies towards religion? Can I honestly be at once a scientist and a Christian; or must I sacrifice one urge in myself to the other? These are the real questions at issue, and they are questions that tear a man in pieces when he faces up to them. And these inner questions reflect themselves outward into conduct and the life of society. Into education, for instance. Is our education designed to develop a scientific or a religious attitude to life? Scientific of course, say some. There is no 'of course' about it— that is mere pride and prejudice. Religious, then? But how and why, and with what result in a world which depends on science and scientific organization? That also is pride and prejudice. Then combine them—a little of each. Precisely! But how do you combine the scientific and the religious outlook in the mind of a child if you cannot combine them in your own? The question has returned upon us. Or, think of its bearing on the problems of sex, marriage and the family; the most urgent problems and the most deep-seated of our own generation. If I approach these questions scientifically, in terms of psychology, biology, eugenics, and so forth, the conclusions I come to, the behaviour I adopt, the reorganization of law and social opinion which I seek are poles apart from those which I should reach and adopt if my approach were religious. That alone is sufficient to show that the question whether science or religion shall predominate will determine the future structure of our social life, and lies at the root of every other problem. It is one which cannot be evaded. To evade it is to decide it both unscientifically and irreligiously. To say that we must look at the problems from both sides is to restate the problem, not to solve it; for how are you to combine conclusions so antagonistic or attitudes so disparate. It is as difficult a problem as the combination of the Wave theory of light with the Quantum theory of energy.

Let us look at one or two of the common formulæ for 'reconciling' science and religion. It is sometimes alleged that science and religion have different fields, that science is appropriate to the study of the material world, while religion deals with the spiritual. This is surely a misconception. I suppose it means that science is a set of beliefs about the material world, and religion a set of beliefs about the spiritual world. But is religion a set of beliefs at all? It is certainly not merely this; and not specially this. To think so would be to confuse religion with theology, i.e. with the science (or pseudo-science, if you like) of the spiritual world. If science is to swallow religion in this fashion, then, I am afraid, religion would speedily go by the board, for science would certainly deny the spiritual world, in any religious sense of the term, altogether. Can you be a scientist and believe in a spiritual world? That is the question. Nor could the spiritual and the material worlds be kept separate, 'cut off with a hatchet', even with the best will in the world. Both meet in the mind of man, and demand to be related. Religion will claim—it cannot help it—that the spiritual world is the real world, and that the truth about this world that matters is the fact that your attitude to it and to life in it determines your place and value in the spiritual world. Religion must claim to control a man's material life; otherwise it becomes a figment of the imagination, and God a hallucination, empty and impotent. Nor can science, even if it would, restrict itself to the material world; it is driven on by an inherent necessity to approach the world of life and of the mind. Biology. and psychology cannot be denied once we admit science at all; and in psychology at least science and religion would have to fight it out or come to terms. Science and religion are not concerned with two different worlds but with one and the same world—the only world there is.

But, it is said, they deal with different aspects of the same world. Science is quantitative, religion is qualitative; that means a difference of method. Science abstracts from the qualities of the world, while it is precisely the qualitative aspect of the world that religion is concerned with. There may be something in this; but as it stands it is clearly false. It might have been maintained with some show of reason until the middle of the last century; but now it is surely groundless. Some sciences, the oldest and most successful, are certainly not concerned with quality. These are the mathematical sciences. But just as surely there are the sciences which are concerned with qualitative aspects of reality—such as biology, psychology, history, sociology and so on. Some of these may not be very successful, but that is no ground for denying that they are sciences. They are products of the scientific attitude of mind and they are after the same kind of truth as the exacter sciences. And further, the qualitative and quantitative aspects of the world are bound up together, inextricably, and the question which is paramount is bound to arise. There cannot be two truths about the same world. Truth is one and indivisible. Is religion to be the science of quality? Then again religion is swallowed by science and disappears.

Similarly, it is impossible to use the old distinction between teleology and mechanism to separate science and religion. You cannot say that science takes no account of the 'purpose of the world'—vague phrase that hides a fog in the mind!—while religion looks upon the world in terms of the purpose of God. That is a controversy within science—the controversy between the vitalists and mechanists in biology. The affirmation of evolution is the affirmation of teleology in the world, and evolution is a scientific, not a religious, idea. The question 'Is there a single purpose in the universe?' is not a religious question. It might quite well be answered in the affirmative by a science which was completely atheistic.

There is one other way of 'reconciling' science and religion to which I shall refer, which has great vogue for the moment in certain quarters, and is really more sensible, though I think ultimately mistaken. The other attempts I have mentioned agree in the strange error of thinking that science and religion are both systems of belief about the world. If that were so, they would arise from the same impulse in the mind, and have the same ultimate aim; they would, in effect, be the same thing; and where they differed one would be right and the other wrong; unless both were wrong together, which is perhaps most likely. But instead of this, we may say that science is rational, while religion is mystical (I suppose that means for the scientists 'irrational'). Or perhaps better, the attitude of science is one of inquiry, while that of religion is one of worship. Now there is obviously something in this. Worship is certainly specifically religious, and it is an attitude of mind which is not compatible with science. Science does not worship. It enquires, analyses, classifies and does sums. On the other hand, religion is not merely worship; and worship may be merely superstitious. If superstitious worship is religion, then astrology and palmistry are sciences. Religion cannot simply sit down and worship anything and everything; it must claim reality for what it worships; and it must make some statement about this reality and assert not merely that it is true but that it is the supreme truth. A religious temper which is indifferent to any truth, scientific or otherwise, is *ipso facto*, superstitious. Religion is not merely the worship of God, but the knowledge of God, for if it does not know its God then God is a figment of the imagination and it worships it knows not what. All honest religion necessarily involves a strenuous effort to know the supreme reality, and the knowledge of God must involve all knowledge in its scope.

Even this is not the most important point. Religion must claim to control practical activity; science need not, and normally does not. To know God involves in its very essence the orientation of life towards God —'bringing every thought into captivity to the knowledge of Christ'—as Paul put it picturesquely. The practice of religion is involved in its knowledge, just as its knowledge is in its worship. It is wrong, therefore, to contrast science and religion in terms of rationalism and mysticism. But if it were *right*, the opposition would be a fundamental and irreconcilable one.

What, then, is the proper distinction between the two? Here we must be on our guard. We must compare them at their best, in terms of their essential and developed nature. We must not compare a full-grown modern science like atomic physics with the religion of a Hottentot, or even of a mediæval saint. The religious man would then properly compare the science of a mediæval alchemist with the religion of Jesus himself. But more than that, we must not credit to science what does not essentially belong to it as science: the honest facing of facts, for example. That may be conspicuous by its absence in modern religion, and by its presence in modern science; but it is not in its nature peculiar to science. It is simply ordinary sincerity, and is demanded in religion just as much as in science. You will remember that I have insisted that science is the one positive expression, up to date, of essential Christianity; and therefore one would expect to find the great human virtues *of the mind* more conspicuous in science than elsewhere, not because it is science but because it is a limited expression of essential religion. We have to compare essential science with essential religion; and I am afraid that means comparing a science that we have got with a religion that we haven't—a science that is Christian with a so-called Christianity that is not.

Science and religion are extremes, and present essentially an extreme contrast.

1. *Science, like art, is fragmentary, while religion is one, like philosophy*. That is not really paradoxical; it means simply that science is a portmanteau name for a set of sciences. I should think that there are as many separate sciences as there are Christian sects. But the sciences are only possible through their separation. It is essential to their existence; while religious sectarianism is religious failure. The scientist is right in reproaching religion with its schisms; the religious man is not right in reproaching science with its multiplicity of sciences. Science must be and ought to be a set of sciences; religion in its very nature is one and ought to manifest itself as one. There is one God; there are many departments of scientific enquiry. And the further science develops, the more fragmentary and specialized in all directions does it become; so that science can never be the knowledge of this or that scientist, while religion is always the religion of this or that man. It is always personal.

2. *Science is abstract, while religion is concrete*. Science must be abstract. It cannot, in its very nature, deal with anything in its individual wholeness. Now, when we talk of the concrete we mean that wholeness

which constitutes the individuality of things. The moment you analyse and classify you are committed to the dissolution of individuality—to breaking things up into their elements. The moment you generalize you are committed to dealing with your subject matter in a special aspect, in terms of what individuals have in common, in contrast to the specific differences which mark their individuality, which make them themselves. This is not an accusation against science; it is its justification. It is the business of science to analyse and classify in general terms; if it fails to be abstract, if it tries to be concrete, it falsifies itself; and, may I add, when scientists forget this they tend to make fools of themselves.

Look at another side of this. Science is general because it is abstract. The general, (sometimes wrongly called the universal,) is its province and its aim. The more general are the laws it discovers, the more general are the truths that it states, the more successful it is, and the better it is pleased. Rightly, for this is its essential business. But this means that science has no concern as science with the individual. Any individual object or person or event is for science merely one of many—an instance, an example, a particular fact illustrating a general rule, known or unknown.

Now if you look at this obvious fact about science you will find that it has certain very curious corollaries. It means, for instance, that science, though it may know everything in general, can know nothing in particular, and reality is always something in particular. It follows that science is not knowledge of reality. Is that startling? It is a commonplace of much philosophy, from Plato to the present day. But in our own time it has been stated by scientists—Professor Eddington, for example. And if we will only put aside the prejudice that science is *par excellence* the knowledge of reality it is really quite obvious at every turn. For instance, science is descriptive, not explanatory. It can say a lot *about* real things in general terms, but there it stops. Or again, science is always seeking objectivity and never finding it. The scientific attitude, faced with a fact, always refers it to something else, some other fact. Again, that is its business. The essential thing for science about anything real—an object or event—is that it is in terms of something else, and that again in terms of something else. There is absolutely nothing for science in the wide universe that is in terms of itself. So science is condemned to chase reality, as it were, round an endless rope, and cannot ever find anything on which to rest. As a result, no scientific statement can ever be final. Its 'truths' exist provisionally and its whole business upon them is to revise them continually. Or, to put it otherwise, science is not itself objective; its business is to invent expressions for the description of reality, and to perfect these expressions.

Let us explore a little further—cautiously. Knowledge is by definition the apprehension of the real—not the description of it, which is another matter. Strictly speaking, therefore, science is not knowledge. I do not say that it is not cognition, but simply that it is not knowledge in the full sense. For example, you cannot know anybody, your father or your friend, by science. The knowledge which we have in mind when we say 'Do you know Keats's *Ode to a Grecian Urn*?' or 'Do you know George Robey?' is knowledge in the strict sense, because it is an objective apprehension of a real individual. And it is just what science does not give us.

3. *Religion is concerned with value; science is not.* The scientific attitude abstracts from emotion. Not merely from bias and prejudice. It strenuously guards against any influence of our emotional nature. That again is obviously its business, and one of its great difficulties. But as a matter of fact, emotion is essential to the grasp of reality—of the concrete individual. Interest is essential to knowledge, and interest is selective. It imposes values, and differential values; and the intenser the interest grows—as it mounts the scale to love—the more it concentrates its selective capacity and so individualizes its object. To be completely general one would have to be completely dis-

interested. But then one could not even be a scientist. One could not even choose between being a psychologist and being a physicist—and it is impossible to be a scientist in general.

Note the corollary of this. Science, in itself, is strictly valueless. That obviously does not mean that science has no value, but that its value is derived from outside itself. It is a relative value, a utility value. This also is true of philosophy. Indeed, it is true of knowledge as a whole. But it is particularly true of science. Science is important as a means to something that isn't science, ultimately to practical activity. The real value of science, and it is immense, lies in the values that it enables us to secure, or to create, in the transformation of human life that it makes possible. Science is essentially and necessarily the servant of life, not its master. And the really important point is that science in itself cannot determine its own proper use. That is a matter of value and of emotion. The pride and prejudice of science, which makes it such a real danger to civilization at the present moment, lies in this; that scientific results can be and will be used for the satisfaction of thoroughly unscientific human passions and desires. And because science cannot determine values or practical ideals, a scientific age is always a materialistic age— *not* because science is materialistic, for it isn't ever, but because a scientific age is an age whose emotions are left uncivilized and barbarous. The civilizing of the emotions is the business of art and religion—of religion particularly, and science cannot do it, because it *must* be free from emotion or cease to be science.

If you object that science satisfies a human instinct, there is a sharp and final answer. First, so does libertinism; and it is unscientific to live by satisfying your instincts. Secondly, the instinct in question must be the instinct of curiosity, and that is not the noblest of human instincts. I simply refuse to degrade science to the level of gossip. If you say: 'No, the instinct for knowledge'—there isn't one: ask any psychologist. If you mean the personal hunger for knowledge, then science does not and cannot satisfy it. Philosophy perhaps, or art, or religion, but not science. The value of science is a utility value, not intrinsic as that of religion is. Science is in fact systematic information, nothing more; and information is for use. That is why it is general. When you want to use something, you don't want to know *it*, only *about* it, what in general it can do. And you will notice that scientific knowledge is always about how things behave, rather than about the things themselves. It is not really important for science to know whether electrons exist or not, so long as things that do exist behave *as if* they were composed of electrons.

4. *Science is impersonal; religion is personal.* Now all

this is summed up in the essence of the contrast between the impersonality of science and the personal character of religion. This is the pith of the whole matter. Whose knowledge is science? Everybody's? Nobody's! Science is impersonal; that is to say, it is available information, and the place for information is in books, where one can find it when one wants it. But even bare information is information for somebody, for some person; the trouble is that no person can make information their own and so turn it into knowledge, without altering its character, colouring it with emotion and experience. That is why science is so much concerned about eliminating the personal factor from its activities and its results. It wants someone who can gain and hold information without personalizing it. This is impossible. Reality is not built that way, and to refuse to face that fact honestly is not scientific; it is pride and prejudice. For after all, science is an activity of persons, it falls within the personal life and must be dominated by it. There is no reason to be ashamed or annoyed by the mystical or poetical or magic power of real language in which personal knowledge expresses itself. For certain personal purposes it is useful and important to depersonalize and dehumanize language and make it merely a means of conveying information—as when we ask a policeman the way. Scientific language is simply real language, the means of personal communication, killed, dissected, and sterilized for laboratory purposes. And the justification of this is that ultimately it serves real personal purposes. Science is an impersonal means to a personal end. Its impersonality is its limitation.

Religion, on the contrary, is unlimited because it is personal. It is the whole unity of reality gathered into the life of a person and so gathering into its own unity all the subordinate aspects of himself. I have not the space to go into detail over this, but must leave you to sketch in this side of the contrast by opposition. Religion is one where science is fragmentary, concrete where science is abstract, concerned with values and so with reality as science is not. Instead, let us notice in conclusion that what started as a contrast of opposites has gradually ceased to be such and religion has become the personal whole of life within which science has its humble but essential place. Science is intellectual understanding, systematic information about the world in which persons live and for their use in living. On that side religion reaches up to the full reality of knowledge, to the knowledge of God; so gathering into one the fragmentariness of science, because God is the unity of the whole; and making that knowledge real because God is individual and concrete—the absolute of personality. But that is only theology, as it were—the intellectual side of religion. And into unity with this religion brings the emotional and the practical sides of human personality; so making man real in his concrete completeness of personal capacity, and setting him in communion with a personal universe.

But, you may well ask in astonishment, where is there such a religion to be found in the world? Look at religion! But I have already insisted on this, and I come back to it in closing. Religion is completely personal; and, therefore, you will only find it where you find a complete and unified personality. That is one side of it; and it takes us back to one or two individuals, to one supremely. But there is another side. For persons are not isolated, and personality is mutual. The personality of Jesus, it seems to me, in realizing the full sweep of religion in himself, created the possibility of its realization as the full life of mankind. We are only at the early stages of the realization of that stupendous work of human personality. And I repeat—the only positive Christian thing in the world as yet is modern science. A Christian philosophy, a Christian art, and then a Christian religion still await creation. A Christian science is impotent without them; and also, because it is Christian, uncontrollable without them, unutilizable in anything like the fullness of power that it gives us. A servant of personality science must be; and if personality remains unchristian, it will use a Christian science for its own destruction. Thus what

I have said is not an attack upon science, but only upon the pride and prejudice that gathers about science to take it by force and make it a king—in order that some men may be rich and powerful and comfortable. These are not the ends of science. My lecture is a defence of science—perhaps even against the scientists—and an attack upon the spurious religion of our so-called Christian culture. It is a demand for a religion that modern science need not be ashamed to serve.

REASON AND RELIGION

RELIGION, in the sense in which it deserves consideration, is one of the three general expressions of rationality. The other two are art and science. Of the three religion is the basic expression and the most comprehensive. The others are more abstract and in a special sense included within religion.

This general statement will be unintelligible if we draw our conception of what religion is from an external and empirical consideration of the historic nature of religious phenomena. Most of these phenomena are infantile and immature. We must look rather at the fields of human experience to which these three expressions of rationality refer and in which they arise. For rationality is objective consciousness, and is possible only in beings who stand in conscious relationship to objects which they know and which are not themselves. Now, there are three general fields in the world to which we stand in such an objectively conscious relation. The objects with which we are concerned may be either material objects, living creatures, or persons like ourselves. It is this threefold character of the objective world which determines the threefold expression of rationality. Science grows out of our rationality in relation to material things. Art grows out of our relation to living beings. Religion grows out of our relation to persons.

Certain obvious implications follow from this. The first is that religion is inherent in our human activities. It cannot disappear. To reject or to deny religion totally is to deny or reject rationality in our relations to other persons. This, however, must not be misunderstood. It is possible, and may be necessary, to reject and disown any particular form or expression of religion which has developed in history. This is not to deny religion. Science is in the same case for the same reason. It is not possible to disown science without denying rationality in the field of our material experience. But it is possible and may be necessary to reject and disown any particular scientific form— be it theory or method or application. And at certain points in human development, the change from one expression of religion into another, like the change from one art-form into another, may be so radical that the continuity of the earlier and later forms is concealed from a superficial examination. Because religion, in some form, is basic and irradicable in human life, it does not follow that our own religious institutions and beliefs, and even what we have come to mean by religion, may not require to be swept away completely in the interest of religion itself. The mature forms of religion may prove to be as unlike our own as these are unlike the religions of primitive mankind. But religion itself can never go, because it is inherent in the human situation. It is an eternal aspect of our rationality.

A further implication is this. Religion is a fuller expression of rationality than either science or art. This follows from the fact that persons are also living creatures, and that living creatures are also material objects. In relation to the contents of the world, science is, therefore, more comprehensive than any other rational expression of our nature. It applies to everything without exception, in so far as it is material, and even persons are at least material bodies. But, on the other hand, religion is more comprehensive as an expression of rationality because, though the relation of a person to other persons defines a limited field, it is a field in which the object includes all the general factors in our experience. In being a relation of person to person, it is also and necessarily a relation of body to body and of living creature to living creature. More than this, since rationality is the defining characteristic of persons, it is only in the full relation of one rational being to another that rationality can completely express its own nature.

Here again a warning against misunderstanding is

necessary. We are comparing things in their meta-physical nature, in terms of their eternal essences, without the limitations imposed by the historical conditions under which they must manifest themselves. To say that in its nature religion is a fuller expression of rationality than science is not to say that contemporary religion is more rational than contemporary science. Quite the reverse. The expression of rationality in science, just because it is less full and complete, must be much easier to accomplish than the expression of rationality in religion. It is inevitable that science should reach a high level of development earlier than religion. Indeed, the expression of our rationality in the human field of the relationships of persons depends upon the prior development of science and art, just as the development of rational thought depends upon the development of the brain and nervous system. It is primarily the development of rationality in science that is revealing the childishness and irrationality of contemporary religion. Humanity is still very young and immature, and our immaturity shows more clearly in the religious field than anywhere else, as it is bound to do. It is much easier to behave as reasonable beings in manipulating wood or stone or metal, than in our dealings with our fellows. What I have said is simply that in their final maturity, whatever forms of expression maturity may demand and produce, religion will necessarily be a fuller expression of our rationality than either art or science. Not more rational, but a fuller expression of rationality. And the reason for asserting this is also the reason for assuming—if it were not otherwise evident— that contemporary religion is less rational than contemporary science. It is simply that the field of experience in which religion expresses our rationality provides a fuller and more comprehensive scope than does the field to which science is by its nature confined.

These rather abstract philosophical considerations enable us to define the nature of religion in its empirical manifestations. In human experience our rationality appears not as a finished product, but as an inherent pressure to rise above irrationality, and thus progressively to achieve our own nature. Religion appears, therefore, as the drive to achieve rationality in our relations with our fellows. This drive is simply the primitive, blind urge to realize our own nature. It is not a conscious purpose. We cannot know, in any explicit way, what our nature is, until it has achieved a satisfactory expression of itself. This also is a point where we should be on our guard and as fully aware as possible of our own limitations. We have a perfect right to define human nature as essentially rational. But we must bear in mind that we have a very meagre notion of what rationality is. The term is not an explicit, analysable notion. It is necessarily vague and confused. In certain fields we can clearly and definitely point to examples, in human activity, of its opposite— irrationality. And we can compare different steps in the development of the individual and of the race and recognize with certainty that one is more rational than another. This is our *point d'appui*. It is probably as far as we can go. And it is on such narrow and exiguous data that any effort to determine with precision what rationality is has to be based. The word 'reason' denotes primarily that which makes the difference between human and sub-human nature. Rationality is the *differentia* of humanity. But when we go on to ask what it is, in detail, that distinguishes human nature from animal nature, we find that we are in a field of inquiry which is largely speculative, and that all answers are partly guesswork. The danger that besets us lies in the fact that it is easier to distinguish rationality from irrationality in the intellectual field than anywhere else. We are apt to define rationality, therefore, in terms of its intellectual expressions and to look upon the characteristic of what is clearly an expression of rationality in this field, as its general characteristic in all fields. This is a highly dangerous and illogical procedure. Whatever is a decisive and determining characteristic of human nature and belongs to human nature alone is, by definition, an expression of rationality. The poetry of Shakespeare, the music of Bach, are obviously as distinctive expressions of the nature of humanity as the philosophy of Plato or the scientific work of Newton; and, therefore, an examination of these to determine, as far as we can, what is being expressed in them, is an inquiry into the nature of rationality. In a word, since what we call genius is, in any field, the fullest expression of human capacity that we know in that field, it must be precisely the clearest and best expression of the nature of rationality. Even in the field of thought rationality is not to be defined in logical terms, since lunatics are often superbly logical. Thought that is merely logical is never rational.

When, then, we insist that religion, in experience, is the pressure towards rationality in our relations with our fellows, we are not handing human relations over to the tender mercies of the logician and the mechanist. Quite the contrary. We are demanding a change in the religious field of the kind which created experimental science out of the empty logical speculation of the mediæval schoolmen. Rationalism is not reason. It is only the intellect in blinkers. Reason is not self-regarding. It is concerned with its object, not with itself; and in the religious field, as much as in the scientific, rationality reveals itself in the capacity to get beyond our individual prejudice, bias and self-interest, and to think and act in terms of a reality that is beyond ourselves and bigger than ourselves.

The first point we have to be clear about is that there is a field of universal human experience which is the religious field. It is the field of personal relationship. The rationality of our nature can only show itself in our behaviour; in the way we relate ourselves actively to our world. There are three fields of relationship. There is the material field, first of all. Our human rationality shows itself in this field in our capacity to make and use tools. Matter becomes an instrument through which we accomplish our purposes. The world becomes material which we appropriate to ourselves. But this is only possible in so far as we relate ourselves to the material world properly, in terms of *its* nature. We have to submit ourselves to the discipline of matter, conform to its laws and demands, if we are to use it for our purposes. Therefore the drive towards rationality in the material field issues, at last, after the failure of all magics and superstitions, in the creation of science, in the patient objective effort to discover the nature of the material world, to understand what its real characteristics are, and what are the inexorable laws of its action. Only in this way can we relate ourselves properly to matter, and use it as our material and our instrument. Science is the sign that we have learned not to pretend that matter is what we would like it to be, not to imagine that it will work miracles for us at a word of command. It is also the sign that we have learned that a patient effort to discover its real nature and to deal with it in terms of its real nature will give us power to use it as our instrument. Through science we relate ourselves *really*, as material bodies, to the material world.

The second field in which we experience the drive to rationality is the field of our own relationship to the world of organic life. We can, of course, treat living nature as an instrument for our purposes, and relate ourselves materially to the world of living creatures; and this has its place. But this is not the full rational relationship of our nature to the organic world. It is a failure to enter into a relationship which is perfectly appropriate, and out of it there can only arise a science of the organic which fails to do justice to its organic nature. Life as life, in its characteristic nature as growth, development, self-reproduction, sensitiveness and instinct, needs another approach. We must find how to relate ourselves organically to organic nature; and the pressure towards an objective, rational relationship with this world of life gives rise to art in all its forms. If it is through science that we come to relate our lives rationally to the material world, it is through art that we can come to relate our lives rationally to the world of organic life. The drive to rationality in this field is a pressure towards balance and rhythm and harmony, towards functional relationship; and the rationality it seeks is a rationality of the instinctive and emotional life. With this field we need not concern ourselves further at the moment, except to observe that the common notion that this is a field of irrationality, that the emotional consciousness is in its nature irrational, is completely false. What is true is that compared with the scientific, material field, our rationality in the organic, artistic field is very feebly developed and still immature and childish. But there is no way in which intellectual rationality can be made a substitute for our failure in the organic field. Beauty is as rational as truth, but it is not possible to incorporate it in human life by any development of intellectual knowledge. The attempt to make scientific rationality the whole of rationality and to look to science to humanize life throughout its whole scope is at once readily comprehensible and radically mischievous. Equally mischievous is the effort of the reactionary to substitute art or religion for science.

But it is with religion that we are concerned, and this definition of the fields of science and art has for its purpose to throw into clear relief the field of religion. When that to which we must relate ourselves is another human being, a person like ourselves, a whole new range of fact, a whole new world of demands confronts us, and the drive to rationality must find an expression for itself which is proper to this new field. It is from this necessity that religion arises as an inherent character of our human situation. There is no escaping from it. It is the central fact of all personal life, and personal life is human life, rational life, the life of objective consciousness.

The primary difference in the relation of persons to persons which distinguishes it *toto caelo* from the other types of relationship is its mutuality. In this case that to which I relate myself is of my own order. The other is my equal, my fellow. If I meet him, he meets me, in the same personal sense. We meet as man to man. This is the basic fact about the objective situation in which one human being relates himself to another. It is no theory, no mystical ideal, but the simplest fact of human experience. And it suffices to define the nature of rationality in human relationships. The drive to rationality in this field is the impulse to achieve equality and fellowship in the relations of persons. Any form of relation between persons which denies personal equality or which obstructs fellowship is irreligious and irrational. Indeed, in this field the two terms mean precisely the same thing. The irrationality is precisely what it is in any field, a failure to behave in terms of the real situation, in terms of the nature of the object. The primary religious assertion is that all men are equal, and that fellowship is the only relation between persons which is fully rational, or fully appropriate to their nature as persons. In this assertion the whole nature of religion is bound up.

The full significance of this will only be apparent if we remind ourselves of certain common characteristics of rationality. Reason is characteristically universal. The universality varies in its nature in different fields, but it is always present. The universality of a work of art is different from that of a scientific formula; but it is still universal in some sense. It has a validity that transcends the particular local and temporal fact of its expression. Religious rationality is equally universal in its nature. Any real fellowship achieved between persons, spills over, as it were, into the desire to share it. It cannot do otherwise. When any fellowship becomes exclusive, it ceases to be a real fellowship and becomes a mere defensive alliance to safeguard common interests. For reason is never self-regarding or subjective. The drive to rationality in the personal field is a drive not merely towards fellowship but towards a universal fellowship, in which all men share. Abstractly stated, this appears in the form that since rationality in the personal field is grounded in the *de facto* equality of men as men, it necessarily demands the fellowship of all persons.

It may strike many readers as strange to define religion without any reference to God. Yet in fact it

is advisable to do so. It is only with the development
of religion that the term 'God' appears, and once it
has appeared the significance of the word is determined, not in any supernatural fashion, but in terms
of the quite human factors we have been discussing.
The idea of God can have no fixed meaning of its
own which is not related to our experience of human
relationships; and it is the significance of the term to
the persons who use it that matters, not the fact that
it is used or refused. When the idea of God has come,
in any particular phase of human development, to
carry a meaning which is in fact false and irrational,
the use of the term will inevitably imply this falsehood. The assertion of the existence of God will be
the assertion of a falsehood, and its denial the denial
of a falsehood. A process of development is always
dialectical and includes negation. When, therefore, a
society has crystallized a conception of God which is
false, the professed atheist may be more truly religious than the theist. For it is the latter who is asserting the existence of something that does not exist.
And we must remember that in human development
a situation often arises where the falsehood of a
traditional conception becomes clear before any
alternative conception which could command rational assent has been discovered. In such a case the
denial of religion may be the only possible course to
take, since all that is known as religion is in fact

shown to be false. This is not of course peculiar to the development of religion. It is a regular feature of the development of rationality in other fields. Most of the great figures of European thought announced themselves as anti-rationalists, or sceptics. Kant is a milestone in the development of rational thought, and a giant among the intellectuals; yet he announced his great work as '*destroying reason to make room for faith*', and dubbed the process of reason '*a dialectic of illusion*'. Nor was he the only opponent of reason whose anti-rationalism proved to be the ground plan of a new understanding of the significance of reason. Science itself, which is the most rational expression man has yet produced, arose as an appeal to fact against the arid speculations of the rationalists of the time. Its experimental empiricism still remains the secret of its own superb rationality.

I do not myself believe that there can be a religion without God, or even that the existence of God can rationally be questioned. But in saying this I mean merely that the universality of reason in the personal field demands an infinite and eternal ground of the particular and limited phenomena of personal experience in the personal field. The point can perhaps be made clear by reference to its analogue in the material field. No scientist could deny without absurdity the existence of matter—though the phenomenon of scientists turned anti-materialist is not unknown in our own day. What they in fact assert when they say that 'Matter does not exist' is really that the prevailing and traditional scientific conception of matter has been shown to be radically false. But what all scientists are bound to assert is that the nature of matter can only be discovered through the observation and determination of particular material phenomena, never by pure speculation about what is contained in the idea of matter. It is the speculative philosopher who discusses matter and defines it. The scientist, who is the man who really knows about matter, is apt to be exceedingly sceptical and impatient over these metaphysical disquisitions. He will assert—surely rightly—that the only way to discover what matter is, is to investigate particular material facts, to deal with actual instances. None of these, of course, *is* matter, because matter is the infinite ground of all instances. It is that which is always expressed and never completely expressed in any particular empirical object. This is at once the ground of the possibility, and of the limitation, of generalization from particular cases. The scientist is thus at once the man who knows most about matter and who talks least about it. He talks instead about the facts—the particular finite phenomena—of the material field. It is similar in the religious field. God is the infinite ground of all finite phenomena in the personal field—and, therefore, ultimately, of all phenomena whatever—but the knowledge of God is possible only through the empirical phenomena of personal relationship. In any particular relationship of persons, if it is truly personal, God is known, as that which is partially, but never completely, realized in it. Thus, like the true scientist, the truly religious man will talk little about God—he will leave that to the speculative philosopher and theologian—and much about the empirical life of personal relationships. He will realize what Blake meant when he wrote: 'God only exists and is in existing beings or men.' So a scientist might truly say that matter only exists and is in existing material phenomena or objects. In particular the really religious man will define the nature of God, not in terms of the analysis of ideas or of transcendental beliefs, but in terms of his empirical knowledge of human relationships. So Jesus is reported to have said: 'He that hath seen me hath seen the Father, and how sayest thou, then, show us the Father.'

We can, therefore, leave this question aside and return to the main point. The field of religious experience is the field of personal relationship. This field is just as empirical and natural as the field of science. The idea of communion with God is the universal correlate of the empirical experience of finite personal relationships and its meaning is discovered and realized only in this empirical field. So

says the New Testament: 'If any man say he love
God and hateth his brother, he is a liar.'

Reason is primarily practical. It is in behaviour
that rationality expresses itself. It is not primarily
reflective or contemplative. Religion, as the expression of rationality in the field of personal relationships is primarily to be discovered in the *behaviour* of
men and women in relation to one another. So far
as they treat one another as equals and enter into
relation as fellows, they are religious or rational. The
theory, or reflective expression of this, whether
scientific, in doctrine, or æsthetic in ritual, is secondary, because it is merely the reflective expression of
these concrete relationships; and like theory in any
field it is valid or invalid with reference to the facts
that it expresses. In particular, the religion of any
society is properly the expression of the forms of
personal relationship which constitute it, of the inter-
personal values which determine its structure. Thus
a society which was in practice completely indivi-
dualist (supposing that such a society could maintain
itself for a moment), would be completely irreligious
or atheistic, however many churches it maintained.
It is not the outward manifestations of religion which
determine whether a society is religious or not. These
may be merely parts of its traditional structure which
persist through habit or because of their political or
economic value, and may have no relation to the

actual nature of the personal relationships between its members by which it lives as a society. In fact, the orthodox religious ritual of any society is always the *symbol* of its structure of personal relationships, and it is this which explains why men who have no religious interests, but have large economic and other secular interests in maintaining the orthodox and traditional structure of their society, can be relied on to rally to the defence of orthodox religion; while men of a religious temper who are concerned to replace the traditional structure by a new one, are apt to find themselves attacking religion.

RELIGIOUS REALITY

THE PHILOSOPHY of religion is not itself necessarily religious. It arises because the philosopher, whatever his personal belief, is faced with a claim which religion makes and cannot avoid making. It is the claim that reality is personal. If that claim is untrue religion is irrational and misleading. If it is true, any philosophy which denies it is false and misleading. The philosopher, if he is to carry out the task which he has set himself of expressing the nature of reality, cannot leave religion out of account. He must evaluate the claim which is implicit in all religious experience and reach some conclusion about its validity. It would seem that in the nature of things this is a claim upon which no compromise is possible. The philosopher must either accept the personal character of the real or he must reject completely the claim of religion to be a necessary and wholesome expression of human nature. If reality is not personal, religion is an illusion. If reality is personal, then any philosophy which describes reality as impersonal or non-personal is false. I cannot see that there is any conceivable alternative. The statement of this antithesis, however, does not convey a simple and unambiguous meaning. Both its main terms—'real' and 'personal'—supply us with marks of interrogation. What do we mean by real? What do we mean by personal? To determine the validity of religion it is necessary to determine the meaning of these terms. What I wish to do in this lecture is to express the results of my own thinking about what personality is, in order to explain what I mean when I accept the religious claim that reality is personal. The question is perhaps the most difficult of all questions, and what I have to say about it is neither final nor satisfactory, but I think that it points in a definite direction which ought to be explored.

For the religious man the choice is equally imperative. He cannot, without compromising his whole position, subscribe to any philosophy that implicitly or explicitly denies that the real is personal. To do so would be to agree that his religious experience was illusory. The attempt to combine the support of religion with the acceptance of an impersonal theory of the universe can only have one result. It must destroy the reality of religion. This attempt is widely prevalent and has been throughout the last century. Schleiermacher, who is sometimes called in Protestant circles the Father of Modern Theology, stated explicitly that as a philosopher he could not accept the personality of God, though the idea might be useful in religious experience, or even necessary to religious life. The result of this view is to concede that religion, in its specifically religious character, is subjective and that, therefore, any attempt to know reality in its objective nature must pass beyond religion and treat it as a phantasy of the child-life of humanity. The atheism of the positivists or of the communists merely asserts honestly the position which a great deal of modern theology implies. They might justifiably quote St. Paul against these theologians and say: 'When we become men we put away childish things.' Any denial of the personality of God is an assertion of atheism.

In the theoretical field the source of this tendency to make religion subjective by denying the personality of God, arises from a misconception of personality. The source of that misconception lies in turn in the dualism of mind and matter which lies at the root of modern thought. That dualism represents the effort to assert the independent reality of matter, although it often appears to be anxious to safeguard the purity of mind. The whole emphasis really falls upon the material side of the dualism. Mind becomes that which is not matter, that which is left over when the reality of matter has been defined.

But theoretical distinctions of such a fundamental character are always the reflections of moral and spiritual debate that is going on in the depths below them. Behind the intellectual dualism of mind and matter lies the much older pagan dualism between body and soul, and in particular the moral form of that dualism which looks upon the body as evil or the source of evil. But this moral dualism is a distinction *within consciousness*, as is evident from the fact that we talk of bodily *desires*. In its developed form it represents the distinction roughly between the intellectual and the emotional aspects of personal consciousness, and an attempt to suppress the latter in favour of an intellectual control of conduct. Into the ramifications of this attitude of mind we need not enter. The point of importance is that any attitude of mind which produces conflict or opposition between two essential elements in personal consciousness, and which seeks to perpetuate the struggle, must be destructive of religion. For whatever else religion may mean it involves at least the effort after the unification of personality and the healing of its divisions. The stress on the intellectual elements and their identification with the good, necessarily leads in the direction of materialism. For the intellect is the instrumental element in our make-up and is concerned in its proper nature with the manipulation of what is material. It is the emotional aspect which is 'spiritual'—as is sufficiently obvious from the predominant place it holds in all artistic, mystical and religious experience. Paradoxical as it may seem, the attitude of mind which sees in the body and the passions a source of evil and something to be subdued by reason is the attitude of mind which is expressed in science, materialism, the love of power and the denial of religion.

The modern philosophical form of the dualism between matter and mind arises from a confusion. The philosopher starts, since the Reformation, from the fact of his own isolated selfhood. He distinguishes himself as thinker from what he thinks about. This is a quite proper distinction within its limits, but it is useless for philosophical purposes. For the distinction is a different distinction for every thinker. When Dr. Schiller draws the distinction, part of what he thinks about is Professor Joachim; but when Professor Joachim distinguishes his thinking from what he thinks about, part of what he thinks about is Dr. Schiller's thinking. To reach a universal distinction on this ground is impossible, and the philosopher must have a universal starting-point. Therefore, he universalizes the distinction by projecting it outwards and so objectifying it. It is then no longer valid. It appears as a distinction between the thinking mind and the object of thought. And that distinction, which is a meaningless one, is soon assimilated to the older distinction between mind and matter. Now, the distinction between mind and matter in this form is a distinction within the field of what is thought about. It is a dichotomy of the world as object. It classifies all the phenomena of experience into phenomena of mind and phenomena of matter. Considered as a classification of phenomena it is obviously a bad one, because it leaves one very important class of phenomena completely out of account. It has no place for the phenomena of organic life. As a result we are driven to attempt to explain all organic phenomena either in terms of mind or in terms of matter, and there arises a ramification of confusion and futile debate from which there is no possible way out. Above all it becomes impossible to think rightly about personality. For behind the dualism there lies the isolation of the individual self which denies the inherent dependence of the individual person upon the society of persons in which he lives and moves and has his being.

To understand the nature of the personal we must get behind the dualism of mind and matter, and the demand for isolation in the individual self which sustains it. (We might note in passing that this demand for isolation expresses the opposition of the individual will to its dependence upon the personal reality in which it exists and is, therefore, the essence of what the theologians call 'sin'.) We can, then, start from two fundamental facts. The first is that our personal consciousness is objective. The second is that the objective world which we know includes three levels of being, the levels of matter, of life, and of personality.

The first of these positions requires further elucidation. To say that personal consciousness is objective is to say that we are persons because we live in and through a knowledge of what is not ourselves. This is the essence of rationality. The difficulty of grasping it arises simply from the fact that it is almost impossible to be explicitly aware of it. There is nothing to contrast it with. But if we consider the familiar statement that 'we live in the world' we shall discover that it is paradoxical. It asserts that we have our conscious being not in ourselves but in what is not ourselves. We live in the other, in that which we recognize to be other. It is only when we withdraw into ourselves and find ourselves in a dream-life of phantasy and imagination that we discover the possibility of a consciousness which has no objectivity, and we discover it precisely because we are now living not in the world but in ourselves, in a world where we are not dependent on reality but masters of the unreal. Our dependence on what is not ourselves—or rather, since we always are dependent, whether we recognize it or not, our recognition of dependence and our living in terms of this recognition—is the core of our reality.

Now let us turn to the second point. The objectivity of our experience reveals a threefold dependence upon the world by revealing three levels of objective reality. We know the world as matter, as life and as personality. This knowledge is the knowledge of a threefold nature in ourselves and of a threefold dependence of ourselves upon the world. We will confine our attention for the moment to the material level. As persons we have an objective consciousness of matter. We know material objects. But this knowledge is inherently a knowledge of ourselves as material objects. It is equally a knowledge of our dependence as material objects upon the society of material objects which is the material world. This knowledge is not primarily a reflective understanding. It is expressed in our conscious activity as parts of the material world. We recognize in every action our dependence as material bodies upon the material world. We live as members of the material world. But this is not a sufficient statement of our nature, for if we were merely material objects in a material world we should not know ourselves even as material objects. Such knowledge presupposes that we already know ourselves as more than material.

But now, if the objective world was merely material, we could not know ourselves as more than material and, therefore, could not know ourselves at all. Our consciousness of ourselves is always a consciousness of what is not ourselves and of our dependence in that relation. We cannot, that is to say, know ourselves except through a knowledge of what is not us, and if what we know as 'other' were merely material we could only know ourselves as material. Unless we know an objective reality which is more than material, we cannot know ourselves at all. For to know ourselves is to be conscious of our personality or selfhood.

The same is true at the level of organic life. We can know ourselves as living beings only through the knowledge of life in the objective world. That knowledge, again, must be our consciousness of living as members of a society of organic beings and in dependence upon it. Its primary form is again not reflective, not a matter of thought and understanding, but a consciousness in action. We live as organisms in a world of life, and our consciousness that we are individual organisms is a consciousness that we belong, as dependent individuals, to a world of organic reality. Yet such knowledge in turn is insufficient to provide for its own possibility. We can only assert our animal nature because we already have a consciousness of ourselves as persons.

In some such way we can be brought to realize that the primary condition of our being is our objective consciousness of a world of personality of which we are members and within which we are dependent individuals. It is in and through my consciousness of other persons alone that I can know myself as a person. And to know oneself as a person and to be a person are the same thing. To be a person is, therefore, to live as member of a personal reality, in dependence upon it.

It is from this point that a constructive beginning can be made. And to do this I should like to formulate the conclusion by stating it in another form. Personality is essentially mutual. There can be no such thing as an isolated person. It is only in relationship between itself and another person that the self can exist at all. Philosophers have continually talked about the self as if it could exist and function in relation to a non-personal world. (This, indeed, is the inner meaning of the dualism between matter and mind.) Even when they have recognized the multiplicity of selves in the world, they have treated them all as different manifestations of the same selfhood. They have thought of themselves standing over against the objective world. 'I and the world' has been their formula. And when they have been constrained to recognize that there are other thinkers besides themselves they have been content, as it were, to multiply the formula, so that it becomes 'I and I and the world'. But obviously the correct formula is 'I and *you* and the world'. This difference between 'I' and 'you' is of the very essence of personality. There is no 'I' without a 'you'. The relationship between persons constitutes their individual personality, and this mutuality of the personal is the basic fact of religion. It is what is expressed by religion in the statement that 'God is Love'. Personality is essentially friendship or the communion of persons.

We must notice, in the next place, that the material and the organic levels of reality are included within the personal. The full existence of a person includes a material and an organic existence. Indeed, it might be more illuminating to point out that the idea of the organic and of the material are, in fact, limitations within our personal consciousness. We do not build up our conception of the personal from our knowledge of the material world. On the contrary, we reach the conception of matter by leaving out certain aspects of our personal experience which we consider to be peculiar to our personal and organic existence. The importance of this consideration is that it indicates that a personal conception of the world includes the organic or the material conception of it. Here again the persistent dualism between mind and matter dogs our footsteps. To assert that the world is spiritual is not to deny that it is material. In a properly personal conception of the world there is no denial of materialism. On the other hand, to assert materialism as the last word about reality is to deny its personal character and, indeed, its organic character.

Now, since personality includes within it an organic and a material nature, there will be three

expressions of personal life, each of which is character-
ized by the objectivity which is the essence of personal
consciousness. The expression of its material nature
is science, in which we must include all those objective activities which are intellectual in character.
These activities arise from the fact that in them personality is in mutual objective relation with the world
as material, and they exhibit their true personal
character in the control of the material world by and
for personality. It is in this sense that the intellect is
essentially instrumental. It is the personal expression
of the instrumental character of material reality.
For this reason also the scientific activities of personality cannot express its full nature. The relationship
of persons to the material world involves necessarily
a limitation of personality to the lowest level of its
real being, and fails to call into activity the capacities
of personal consciousness which lie above this level.
The second expression of personality, which corresponds to its organic nature, is art. It is the expression
of the objective and mutual nature of personal consciousness in relation to the organic nature of the
world. And since that which is alive is also material,
this second activity includes the scientific activity
within it. To put it otherwise, the relation between a
person and what is alive in the world calls into
activity all the capacities of consciousness which are
aroused by material reality together with new

capacities which lie dormant in the relationship with matter. For these new activities the vague term feeling is perhaps the most usual expression. They are the activities through which we are aware at once of life in the world and in ourselves. But at this level also the full nature of personality is unrevealed. The object in the relationship, because it is less than personal, is incapable of calling into action the whole capacity of personal consciousness. This can only be expressed when the 'other' in the mutual objective relationship is itself personal. Only then does like meet like and result in a relationship of equals in which the expression of personality can meet a response in the world at its own level of being. Under these conditions alone can personality express itself in its wholeness and be fully related to the world. This field in which all the capacities of personality are expressed in a mutual, objective relationship with that which is not itself is the field of religion.

There is, then, a definite field of empirical experience which is the field of religion. It is the field of personal life—not, of course, the field of individual isolation. When Professor Whitehead says that religion is what a man does with his solitariness he is saying what is almost the reverse of the truth; although he is, unlike many philosophers, moving in the right universe of discourse. Religion is what a man makes of his personal relationships. This field of personal relationships is the centre of every human life. That is a mere statement of fact. But it does not follow that every human life realizes its religious nature. In his personal relationships a man is in the field of religion. Whether he achieves reality in this field depends on whether he is able to achieve objectivity and mutuality. We may live in relation to other persons as if the relation were not a personal one. It always *is* personal, whatever we do about it. But we may behave as if it were not. All failure of this kind is a failure to realize in action—and, consequently, in reflection—the real nature of the relationship between persons. It involves the loss of personal objectivity. In relation to another person we isolate ourselves and so fall into subjectivity and become individualists. When that happens, the relationship is treated in action and in thought as of a sub-personal type. There are two possibilities. One is that the relation is treated as of the material type; in which case the other individual is treated as an instrument or a means. Slavery is the crudest form of this type of unreality in personal relationships, but it includes any relationship in which individuals use one another as instruments. The second type of unreality falsifies the personal relationship by making it organic. In that case the relationship is treated as functional and becomes a co-operation for the achievement of a common purpose. Any conception of human relationships which grounds them upon the existence of a common purpose which each serves in his own way involves unreality of this type. Such conceptions of human relationships are properly described as irreligious, because they deny the reality of the relationship as a communion of persons. It is not enough to insist that human nature is essentially social, since society may take any of these forms. What makes the society real is that the relations between the persons concerned are essentially religious, that is to say, grounded in mutual communion, and the equality which this implies. For, without equality, there can be no mutuality. I do not mean, of course, that in a true society organic and material relationships between persons are non-existent, but only that they are dependent relations falling within and grounded in the relation of friendship. The material and the organic are unreal in independence. Their reality lies in their dependence upon the personal and their inclusion within it.

So far I have made no mention of God. This is because I think it more important to define first that field of purely human experience which is the field of religious consciousness. The dualism of mind and matter reflects itself all too easily in the dualism between secular and sacred, natural and supernatural, the human and the divine. The result is that we think of God as isolated from the world and, therefore, that the religious life involves a turning away from man to God, from this world to another world, so that religion becomes something apart instead of the fundamental activity of human life. But now, having made that point clear, I should like to indicate in closing how essential to the view that I have outlined is the idea of God. All experience at any level is the experience of the finite in the infinite. Even a triangle, as Spinoza pointed out, can only be seen, or imagined, as a limitation of infinite space. At the material level we apprehend all material objects as finite and dependent upon the material infinite. This is not matter of reflection but of immediate common experience. Similarly we apprehend all organisms as finite dependents of infinite life. And when we come to the personal field it is no different. I have already insisted that our apprehension of ourselves as persons is at the same time an apprehension of our dependence upon what is not ourselves. We can now see that it is an apprehension of our own dependence and the dependence of all other finite persons upon infinite personality. God as infinite personality is the primary natural experience of all persons. One might almost say, if it were not for the traditional limitation of our use of language, that God is the first perception.

That, then, is my philosophy of religion. Its concrete, practical meaning I can indicate in a few

words. It is not a reflective formulation of religion
as we know it, though it owes much to the history of
European religion and more to the manifestation of
religion in great religious men and in Jesus supremely.
It is rather a demand for a new step in the creation
of human society. The field of the personal, which is
the field of religion, is one where we grope in the
dark and in which our civilization is perilously un-
skilled. In that field the modern world remains a
world of individualism. Individualism involves the
isolation of selves and the denial of community. It is
therefore anti-religious. Our religious life remains
primitive, instinctive and undeveloped. The religious
task remains unfulfilled. Its goal is the creation of a
human society, universal in its extent, based upon
the communion of persons. Until we envisage this as
the mission of religion we shall continue to rely upon
force and fear and fraud to maintain an appearance
of social unity. We have to address ourselves to the
task of creating the life of truly personal relationship
between men, and of destroying those elements in
modern society which frustrate and deny it. Whatever works for this end is religious. Whatever opposes
it is the enemy of religion.

THE MATURITY OF RELIGION

I

I AM CONCERNED in this lecture with development in religion. It will be wise, therefore, to begin by noticing that there is a sense, and a true sense, in which religion is eternal and unchanging. Religion in development is man in search of God throughout history, building into a fuller religious life the experience of the past. But religion is also the consciousness of life in God; that which we seek for is also there always and eternally in us. It is this eternal aspect of religion which is expressed in the religious recognition of equality in all human life at any stage of its development; in the knowledge that all distinction of superiority and inferiority are relative distinctions; and that ultimately all persons and all personal experience are of equal, because of eternal or infinite, worth. Just so in love between two persons, if it is a real love, there is a sense in which it is always perfect and complete, and this, as we know very well, is not in contradiction with the fact of development in that love; it is, indeed, the condition of the development.

Here we are concerned with the development of religion as it falls within the eternity of religion, conditioned by its eternity. We are also concerned with the reality of this; with *real* religion. For not everything that appears to be religious is so. There are many things that masquerade as religion and are, in fact, something else. There are often, for example, political or economic motives for maintaining an old religious form, when it no longer expresses any religious experience. Such religion is just not religion at all. It is really politics or economics masquerading as religion. There is, therefore, a distinction to be drawn between real and unreal religion at any stage in the development of religion. But also within real religion there is an interpenetration of reality and unreality, which is a completely different phenomenon. This is essential to the development of religion. Development in religion is a temporal process in which it is gradually made real, or in which it gradually realizes itself. It is, at any stage, real religion incompletely realized and, therefore, falsified in its expression. Through the process of development religion finds its own meaning more completely, and expresses that meaning more really, with less falsification. To revert for a moment to the eternal aspect, there is a perfection of religious experience possible at any stage in the development of religion, though it is exceedingly rare at any stage. The religious experience of Isaiah may be perfect and yet express a stage of religious development which is far from complete. And my own religious experience may be very imperfect compared with that of Isaiah and yet belong to a much completer stage in the development of religion. So a person may be much more complete and perfect as a child or an adolescent than he ever succeeds in being as an adult; and this does not contradict the fact that childhood is human nature incompletely developed.

All this is introductory. But now we must draw our first distinction of importance within the field we are considering. It is the distinction between immaturity and maturity. This is a distinction within development, that is characteristic of all development. It draws a line of division between two stages in all development, between the development *to* the mature form, and the development *of* the mature form when it has been reached. In the stage of immaturity the full nature of the growing thing has not yet expressed itself. Its essential character has not yet declared itself or become apparent. When maturity is reached the real nature of what is implicit in the immature stages has declared itself and can be apprehended. Then only can the earlier stages be comprehended in terms of what has shown itself as their real meaning. But, on the other hand, life does not end at the point when maturity is reached. Properly speaking, it begins there. There is a development of the real nature which has declared itself which can only begin when its maturity has been reached. We continually speak of development as if it consisted only in the first stage, as if growth was completed when maturity is reached. This is not so. The growth of the mature organism is the real development to which the earlier stages were only a necessary prologue. I am reminded here of the statement of Marx, that with the achievement of communism prehistory would come to an end and history would begin. For history is the development of mankind, and its first stage is the development of man to maturity—up to the point where personal nature has declared itself. Only thereafter can the real history of man as man begin, in place of the prehistory of man in the making.

What distinguishes the development of mankind from all other forms of development is its dependence upon consciousness. It is not true that our development consists in the development of consciousness. That is the fallacy of idealism. It is rather that our life remains subhuman or immature so long as we do not know what we are doing or why we are doing it. It is only through living, in the stages of our immaturity, that we gradually become conscious of the personal nature that is developing in us. We cannot become conscious first and then begin to live. But the development of that consciousness of our personal nature through the successive stages of immaturity is itself an essential part of our development. The development from one stage to the next depends upon the consciousness of ourselves as we were at the earlier stage. For human development is the development not of consciousness but of conscious life. The maturity of man is a conscious maturity. Human life cannot be mature until it is conscious of its own maturity, that is to say until it has become fully conscious of its real nature, and begins to live in that consciousness. In that sense human development must wait upon the development of consciousness. Until we know ourselves we cannot be ourselves.

One other general point about development requires to be noticed. In any process of growth to maturity different elements reach maturity at different stages. The basic functions must be completely matured before the secondary or higher functions can develop to maturity. For example, the processes of metabolism in any organism must reach their mature stage before the processes of reproduction can mature. But the developing organism does not reach maturity until all the functions have reached maturity, and the whole of them have been maturely integrated. When we apply this to human development we realize something of great importance. The basic aspects and functions of conscious life must reach maturity first; and these are the least characteristic of human life as such. I will give one example only, which we may find of special help in thinking about the maturity of religion. Our consciousness of ourselves in the material world must reach maturity before our consciousness of ourselves can mature on the higher planes of our being. Science must reach maturity before art or religion can. We must win through to the knowledge of ourselves first upon the material plane; for that is a condition of reaching a mature self-knowledge upon the organic and the personal planes. Any effort to resist the development of a true materialism in the interests of 'spiritual' development is indirectly an effort to prevent the development of a mature spirituality. When religion fights science, it fights itself. So the young artist who seeks to escape the material responsibilities of earning a living and supporting a wife and family in order to be free to devote himself to his art is really cutting himself off from the possibility of his own artistic development.

Now we may turn to religion itself and consider its development in the light of these general characteristics of human development. On its inner side, religion is the impulse in human nature to enter into communion with the world, the demand for conscious community with all that is not itself. If we compare it in this inner sense with science and art, we see that science is the impulse to control, and art the impulse to appreciate, all that is not ourselves. It is this that sets the limits of art and science. It limits science to the material field, which is, in fact, the whole of that which could be controlled by conscious life. The effort to control life or spirit is a sign of immaturity. In immature religion there is a constant effort to control the divine by magic or incantation or prayer and ritual. This means that human life has not yet reached maturity in the scientific field, so that the scientific impulse intrudes into a sphere of experience where it is irrational. Art, too, in its immaturity, is ignorant of its limits, ignorant that in the personal field appreciation is a blasphemy if it stops at appreciation and refuses communion. It is communion in conscious community which is the key-word of religion; and the development of religion to maturity is the conscious realization of this as the real nature of the religious impulse. Once religion has reached the point at which it has grasped, in its full scope and implications, that this is its real demand and its real nature, religion has reached maturity, and we can then begin to live the developing life of religious maturity.

We can only understand the immaturity of religion, so far as we are yet able to understand it, when we have grasped this. Immature religion cannot understand itself, because it has not yet grasped this as the essence of its own impulse. We can at once realize that religion is essentially concerned with society—with the expression and the creation of community. Indeed, the development of religion to maturity is the story of the groping efforts of men to realize the social nature of their own being. The process, because it goes on under the impulse of a blind pressure in men and women, takes the most perverse and irrational forms. Often it has taken the form of bloody efforts to exterminate all those who are not in the community, so as to leave only the one community in being. Often it has expressed itself in sexual orgies—because sex is the most intimate expression of communion between two human beings in their organic nature. Religious symbols are symbols of communion, and religious rituals are expressions of communion, in however limited a fashion communion may be conceived.

It is important also to recognize that this demand for communion which is the religious impulse in man, is necessarily absolute. It is without limits. It comes into operation wherever there is the absence of complete community. It cannot be satisfied within limits. It must realize itself universally or remain unrealized and unsatisfied. This dictates its goal, which can be nothing short of the complete integration of all human beings in community and of humanity with the world in which it lives. But in the time process towards this unrecognized goal there are contradictions which arise. The pressure towards complete communion has many aspects. We may find that completeness in one direction makes for incompleteness in another. If communion extends to a large number of persons its inner completeness—its intensity—may tend to be lost. We may seek to achieve an inner completeness of communion by limiting the number of the elect, and excluding all others from the fold. We may seek to gain a greater universality by confining communion to one aspect of life—to the spiritual aspect, for example, as distinct from the material aspect. None of these efforts to set limits to the complete community that the religious nature of humanity demands can ever be maintained; though in the process of development it may often be necessary to set temporary limits on one side in order that there may be development towards a greater completeness on another. The exclusiveness of the Greek city-state community was necessary to the realization of an inner intensity of communion. When that process had gone as far as it could go within these limits, the exclusiveness had to go in face of the religious impulse to the greater inclusiveness of the Macedonian and then of the Roman Empire.

But we are not concerned with the development of religion in its full scope, only with the difference between its immaturity and its maturity. One aspect of the development is of special importance to us, because it belongs to the nature of religion alone, or in a peculiar sense. The development of religion is in its substance the integration of human society. In a very real sense, the development of religion is the development of human society to its full universal integrity. But human life **is** conscious life, and consciousness is achieved first in individuals. Here lies the task of the religious genius. He is the individual in whom the consciousness of the meaning of religion is achieved at any stage in human development and through whom it is mediated and made available to humanity as a whole. He is indeed the mediator between God and man. He is the interpreter to any society of men of the stage of community which they have achieved. He is the Word that expresses, and so realizes in consciousness, for others as well as for himself, the meaning of the religious impulse as it has expressed itself in the creation of community. That consciousness, that expression in the world of the prophet, is the condition of any further advance in the achievement of community. It turns mere community into conscious community or communion, and in doing so sets life free for a fuller achievement. But now the condition of this further achievement depends not merely upon the consciousness of the religious genius, but upon the sharing of that consciousness by his society. He has to be accepted by them; his realization has to become, through him, their realization. His experience has to become a shared experience, the common experience of the society. Only then can a new social integration begin; and in the later stages this propagation of the religious experience of an individual may take long periods of time, and be itself a long development in the consciousness of men. For there is one characteristic of the realization in consciousness of any particular experience; it is generalized. In becoming conscious of the significance of the community which has been realized in his own society, the religious genius removes the limitations of its particularity, and makes it available, not merely for his own but for a wider society. In the development of religion as a whole, there comes a point at which the *full* significance of the religious impulse is realized by one individual human being, and so becomes universally available for all men. He can then realize consciously —in idea—the complete nature of the religious life, the full meaning of the religious impulse in man. This, to my mind, is the significance of the personality of Jesus in history. He was the religious genius who realized the meaning of the community achieved through their history by his own people—the Hebrew race; and in realizing it he made available the universal meaning of religion for all time and all people.

But this does not mean that the maturity of religion was reached in Jesus. On its individual side, the religious experience of Jesus was complete and mature. But religion itself had not reached maturity. That could only be through the building of a community in which the realization of the meaning of the religious impulse which Jesus secured had become a common realization. Throughout the Christian era religion in Europe developed towards a common and shared realization of the significance of religion which Jesus discovered and expressed. Its stages are stages in a progressive realization of Jesus by society, and each fresh realization involves the rejection of earlier, more partial and inadequate realizations. They are reached, as all stages in the development of religion are reached, through a social integration in European history which alone enables individuals to discover, in the experience of the societies to which they belong, a new significance in the life and teaching of Jesus. Such a realization must itself be religious, not theoretical; and I might remark in passing that what distinguishes a religious understanding from a merely intellectual one is that the former is not merely an understanding of the teaching of Jesus or its development by others, but an understanding of oneself and one's own experience in the light of that.

It is this process of sharing, through personal social experience, in the realization of the religious revelation of Jesus that is characteristic of the development of European religion. The emphasis in it falls upon the development of social consciousness, and it is this which causes the division between the secular and the sacred, the opposition of materialism and idealism, the dualism of mind and body in our history. The maturity of religion waits on the development of consciousness, upon the universal sharing of a maturity of consciousness which has been already achieved as the individual consciousness of one religious genius. Religion has not yet reached maturity among men because we have not yet understood Jesus, and the mark of its immaturity in particular is its separatedness from temporal life, its backward-looking temper, its continual quest for its own meaning, its incapacity to do the specific task of religion, to integrate the community of mankind.

THE MATURITY OF RELIGION

II

THIS ANALYSIS of religion in its process to maturity requires to be supplemented by a more concrete statement which would contrast immature religion with mature religion. I shall try to indicate, therefore, what I think would be the main differences between the mature religion of the future and religion as we have known it. It may be helpful to look at a subordinate aspect of human experience which has already reached maturity—I mean science. Science found its real nature at the Renaissance, and that maturing of science is closely bound up with the Protestant Reformation. Yet the scientific impulse is as old as man. It is the impulse to control nature through understanding. That impulse has had its own growth to maturity and in the light of science in its maturity earlier expressions are seen to be misunderstandings, often of a most grotesque and ridiculous kind. If we try to discover in what the difference between mature science and its immature forms consists, we find the essence of it in a new attitude of mind which defines a new method and secures unity and continuity of development through a full consciousness of the task. There is first a repudiation of dogmatism, and a conviction of ignorance. Immature science, like immature religion, is cocksure and convinced of its knowledge. Mature science is humble and tentative, convinced of the immensity of its ignorance, and sure only that patient research can gradually extend the field of knowledge. It has given up the hope of certainty; it has lost its life in order to save it. It has become objective, governed by the facts, submitting to the discipline of the world it seeks to know. It has, in fact, become experimental and empirical, instead of speculative and intuitive. It knows what it is after, and what are the conditions of achievement. Above all, it has found the field of concrete experience with which it is concerned, and so has a simple, concrete test for the reality of its hypotheses and ideas. If your notion is true, it enables you to control the world, to do something through understanding. It brings body and mind together in action. That is the essence of experiment. No longer do you divide the schools in speculative debate on the question whether a stone dropped from the mast of a moving ship will fall at the foot of the mast or not. You climb the mast and drop the stone and so settle the question once for all. In doing this you discover that all the fury of debate only proved that nobody was really interested in the question they were debating. They were only interested in maintaining their own opinion against their rivals'. They were all afraid to make the experiment, in case they should discover that they were wrong. So the divorce between ideas and things persisted, until someone had the courage to doubt his own opinion and accept the simple practical test.

With the will to experiment, science came to maturity, and the change swept away all the old speculative childish science, and created something completely new. Henceforward the least intelligent of scientific practitioners was greater than the greatest of the speculative intellects. So Jesus, in the maturity of his own religious understanding, said: 'I say unto you, among them that are born of women there hath not risen a greater than John the Baptist; notwithstanding, he that is the least in the Kingdom of Heaven is greater than he.'

Now it is precisely here that I find the marks of immaturity in our religious experience. It remains intuitive and speculative, severing the spiritual field from the material, interested in maintaining the certainty of its various faiths, rather than in discovering their feebleness and falsity in the face of facts. It remains blind to the concrete field of human experience to which it refers, and incapable, indeed afraid, of exercising control in its own sphere. It remains uncreative and on the defensive, the champion of an old tradition, not the way into abundant life. Religion will become mature only through recognizing its own real nature instead of attempting to offer pseudo-satisfaction for a demand in us which it does not understand. When it becomes mature it will put away such childish things. The religious demand is a demand for universal communion in a universal community. Mature religion would be the satisfaction of this demand through the creation of communion, and of community as the condition of communion.

We find in Jesus the paradigm of this coming to maturity of the religious consciousness in man. What did it mean for Him? It meant straight away that he recognized his mission as the establishment of the Kingdom of God among men, the creation of the Kingdom of Heaven on earth. It meant that he became clearly conscious of the methods by which this was possible. He accepted, that is to say, the task of a social revolutionary—to establish among men a new and universally human social order. But he realized this as the religious task of creating a universal communion among men, and not merely as the task of creating a new social form. This realization dictated his method of revolution. It ruled out certain methods as ineffective for the creation of communion. It did not rule out any sphere of life from the scope of the revolution. The task was no other-worldly task. It was not the creation of the Kingdom of Heaven in Heaven. There was nothing mystical or peculiarly 'spiritual' in it. It was the task of creating conscious community among all men everywhere—nothing less; and it necessarily included all the conditions, economic, political and personal, which are involved in this. Nor is this any special or particular task. It follows immediately from the realization of the significance of the religious nature of man, as the task of mature religion.

There are three features of the contrast between the mature conception of religion and religion as we know it to which I wish to draw attention. Mature religion is all-inclusive, it is concrete and it is creative. It is in the first place all-inclusive in contrast with the limited character of contemporary religion. For us religion is one aspect of human experience, contrasted with others, such as the scientific or the artistic, the political or the economic. Mature religion would not stand in contrast to these: it would include them. The distinction that we draw between the religious life and the secular life would simply seem grotesque. The question whether religion should or should not interfere in politics would be meaningless. For religion is not an aspect of life which can be contrasted with other aspects; it is the integration of all aspects in one whole. Every aspect of life arises from one or other of the elements which make up our complex human nature, and religion is the integrity of the whole man in his eternal li.e. These two things —the inner integrity of the individual and his integration in communion with all individuals—are strictly correlative, since human nature is objective and can only be integral in the integrity of its relationship to what is not itself. Similarly, there could be no distinction between religion as communion with God, and the social community of man. There can be no whole without its parts; and a communion with God which is not a communion with man is no communion at all, but its refusal. 'If any man say he loves God and loveth not his brother, he is a liar, and the truth is not in him.' For religion in its maturity whatever is a condition of real and complete communion between men is a condition of religion itself.

It is in this sense that I believe that mature religion will be concrete. It will recognize the facts of our common human experience on which it is based and to which it refers. It will have lost the impulse to other-worldliness—the impulse to substitute for the immediate expression of the infinite in our everyday life a separate and therefore an ideal or imaginary world to which it can refer its impulses and intentions. Undoubtedly religion belongs to another world

than the world of science and art, of economic and
political action. But that is merely because these
worlds are not real worlds at all but only abstract
partialities, severed from the full world of our daily
experience—the real world, which is a personal world
because we are persons and our nature is a personal
nature, its demands and its satisfactions personal
demands and personal satisfactions. It is amazing
how blind we are to this simplest and commonest of
all our fields of experience, and to the manner in
which it determines and conditions all the others.
The last thing we seem to become aware of in our
conscious reflection is one another and the concrete
ties that bind us together in the bundle of life. 'What
is he?' we tend to ask about a stranger, and we expect
an answer in terms of a business occupation, or a
profession or a social position. If we were answered
that he is a man of such-and-such personal quality
we should feel that we had been cheated. Yet it
would be the real answer to the question.

For religion to become concrete would mean that
its interest became an interest not in the cherishing
and fostering of religious feelings and ideas in us, but
in communion with persons—real flesh and blood
persons—in our actual world. The religious life would
thus become the life of actual communion between
people; the sharing of our lives with others. Its aim
would be to increase the depth and completeness

and universality of direct personal relationships, to make love the universal and actual reality of our lives. Its task would be an experimental task—the task of discovering, in experience, the conditions of complete personal communion, of abolishing all the hindrances to its development in depth and breadth.

It would be ridiculous to suggest that religious activities as we know them are of this concrete kind. When we gather together for religious purposes we do not enter into communion with one another, except in idea and feeling. We do not actually share our concrete lives. At the best we achieve the symbolic expression of a communion which might be between us and is not. Yet it rarely occurs to us that this feeling of being one in a religious communion refers to the concrete actuality of our daily lives. It remains purely ideal and unreal. And it must do so until it becomes a material sharing of our material substance. Until our material possessions are at the disposal of all those with whom we are in communion for their need, it is idle to talk of sharing our lives, or of having the reality of our lives in common. A mature religion would simply take this idea and sense of community and make it real by building it into the actual structure of human life on every plane. It would be the substantiating, the materialization of religion as we know it. The spiritual world would cease to be an ideal world—other than the material world. It would become the material world itself raised to a higher power, integrated in a new unity of personal life.

Lastly, the effect of this materialization of religion, through which it finds the world of fact to which it belongs, would be that religion would become creative. In its immaturity religion is not creative, except of images and ideas and symbols. What makes religion such a conservative force is not that in its real nature it is conservative, but that as yet it is immature. It remains in the child stage of imitative action and play. It has not become serious and responsible. It does not yet carry its ideas into action. We still think of the religious man as one who conforms to ancient practices, or who holds fast to certain traditional beliefs, or at best as one who has a vivid consciousness of the Eternal, who communes with God by communing with his own soul. We should never imagine that a scientist was a man who devoured all the books of the great scientists of the past, and knew all about the latest theories. A scientist is a man engaged in the discovery of what is unknown, who extends our knowledge of the world and so increases our control over it. Neither would we call a man an artist because of his archeological scholarship in the field of art, nor even because of his skill as a copyist. An artist is one who creates new visions of beauty hitherto unguessed. Surely a religious man must be one who creates in the religious field—who understands and reveals what has been hitherto hidden and secret, and who creates new possibilities of communion, who integrates human society in new forms of shared experience, who experiments in the world of human community and discovers the conditions and the methods of new and deeper intimacies between man and man, and between man and the world. Until in this way religion becomes a force for the creation of community, of the conscious community of men and women who know and appreciate and love one another, not merely religion, but the life of mankind is immature and sub-rational. For all our rational investigation and rational planning of the economic and political and social spheres is without meaning unless it is the means to one end—the living of the personal life of community in joy and freedom. To sacrifice life to its own conditions is the ultimate insincerity and the real denial of God.

Perhaps I may sum this up most concretely by focussing your attention upon its institutional aspect. It follows from what I have been trying to say that we have only one recognized institution which is truly religious; and that is not the church but the family. Churches are really political institutions in the widest sense—or perhaps one might call them social clubs of those whose interest in religion is alive. I am not trying to slander or to criticize churches in saying this—I am referring to churches at their best. I mean that they are organizations for a specialized social function, not integrations of human life in its full personal character. They are really peculiar to the stage of religious immaturity in which the mature conception of religion which Jesus had is being propagated and becoming a social conception, shared by mankind. But the family is religious in its essence, and it comes to maturity when it comes to be based upon free choice. I say it is religious because its unity rests upon personal affection and covers every aspect of personality. It only comes into existence through marriage. The fact that a man and woman love one another does not constitute marriage. Such love is ideal or spiritual. Until that love integrates their lives, socially and materially, so that it produces a sharing of material goods and a concrete unity of life, there is no marriage, there is no formation of a family. So soon as the love is implemented by the community of property and of material life, the family is born, two persons are integrated in communion in their full personal nature, and the development of a family begins. And it is this that makes the family the nucleus of human society, the centre of reference of all social, economic and political institutions, so that Aristotle could insist that the State did not consist of individuals but of families united in a larger polity.

But the family as we know it is failing; largely because it has become inadequate to the social and economic life of our time. Because it is immature our religion can only complain helplessly and seek by exhortations and pleadings to maintain the family. It cannot create religious institutions adequate to the task which is demanded of the family as we have it. It has not even seen yet that there precisely lies its task. For the family as we have it to-day, consisting of one man and one woman and two or three children, is called upon to bear a burden of responsibility which it simply cannot carry. It is our *only* religious institution, and it is called upon to do the whole gigantic task of integrating persons in a love-unity which is not merely ideal but concrete and creative. In simpler and more primitive times, when the task was much easier, the family was much larger and more complex. But it was mainly on a basis of blood-relationship eked out by slavery. It is its development towards maturity which has reduced it to such a narrow and ineffectual compass—the effort to reach the point at which it could be based upon the free personal choice of equal partners. It needs, I think, to develop in size—not in the number of children, but in the number of adults which it unites, in the freedom of choice which it has achieved. This is, perhaps, the centre of the task of mature religion in our time. It is the task of creating forms of personal community, not of a purely spiritual or ideal kind, but of a concrete and material kind, of creating in fact new religious institutions. I am using this as an illustration of my whole meaning, though it is much more than an illustration. And the central point which it illustrates is this. Religion is, indeed, spiritual. But the spiritual is not other than the material, but inclusive of it. Spirit is not other than body but more than body. And any effort to establish a spiritual life which is not a material life, any effort to have a religion which does not include and integrate the material aspects of our being, by integrating us with one another in a unity of material life, is an illusion, and a symptom of the immaturity of our religion. Till we have overcome this dualism of Spirit and Matter —not by denying either but by integrating the two in an inseparable wholeness—religion will never know itself or begin its development in maturity. 'Whoso hath this world's goods and seeth his brother have need and shutteth up his bowels of compassion from him, how dwelleth the love of God in him?'

THE CONSERVATION OF PERSONALITY[1]

IN A series of annual lectures delivered by different persons upon the same theme, it would seem proper that each lecturer should approach the subject in the way which his special training or aptitude marks out for him. I have sought therefore to make my contribution to the purpose of the Drew Lectureship as a philosopher, and to limit myself, in my discussion of immortality, to that aspect upon which philosophy may have a contribution to make. To me this means, in particular, the combination of the widest sympathy with all aspects of human effort that can be achieved, with as strict and unprejudiced a judgment as I am capable of. This seems to entail the recognition that religion is an essential and fundamental activity of human life, in some sense more fundamental and more inclusive than any other, and that Christianity in particular, however much it may be, in its familiar expressions, infected with

[1] Drew Lecture on Immortality. 1932. Reprinted from the *Congregational Quarterly*, January 1933.

subjectivity and incapable of expressing its true nature, is the only form of religion known to us which contains within it the germs of a possible universality and is, therefore, the only religion which can claim with any significance the capacity to determine the community of all mankind. No other religion, it seems to me, could possibly face the full light of rational criticism based upon our developing science without being destroyed. Christianity, while it cannot emerge from that ordeal unchanged, yet holds within it the capacity of transformation, of a transformation, indeed, which would be the realization of its inherent nature.

On the other hand, it is not clear that a belief in the immortality of the soul is essential to the religious or even to the Christian consciousness. By this I mean merely that if it were possible conclusively to disprove personal immortality, that would not mean, *ipso facto*, the end of Christianity or of religion. Even if it did it would be incumbent upon us to stand by the truth as we discovered it. The philosopher, at least, must demand the liberty to approach this question with an open mind.

The prevalence of the belief in immortality throughout history, and among peoples of the most diverse types, is in itself no argument for the truth of the belief. For many of our beliefs are the product either of the limitations of our knowledge or of our hopes and fears. The former kind, if they are false, are gradually dissipated by the progress of knowledge. But beliefs which have their basis in hopes and fears which are universal are not so easily tested. And only the constant watchfulness of self-criticism continually renewed can serve as a protection against self-deception. In some sense, it would seem, the desire for immortality is and has always been very widespread. It is not necessarily, nor even primarily, a selfish desire. More often it is a desire for the immortality of others from whom death has separated us, for the opportunity to recapture and re-establish those supreme values in life which death destroys. But much deeper than the hope of a possible extension of life beyond the grave lies the universal fear of the actuality of death. The gift of reason brings with it, inescapably, the knowledge of death. And this knowledge has to be reckoned with if it is not to paralyse activity and generate an overmastering despair.

One means of escaping from fear and its paralysing effects is to succeed in ignoring or denying its object; and there can be no doubt that to a considerable extent the belief in immortality arises in this way; that it performs the function of a psychological defence-mechanism by denying in idea the fact of death and so enabling men to ignore it in their actual life. I do not contend that this is an explanation of the belief in immortality, certainly not that it is a complete or adequate explanation. But that it is a factor that is often present, and may always be present, it would be unreasonable to deny. If we are seeking the truth we shall have to reckon with it and be on our guard against it, since its subjective nature provides us with the wish to prove the truth of immortality and offers not even the slightest evidence for its truth. In any enquiry where our secret desires are inevitably engaged, we are continually in the danger of weighting the evidence in their favour, and it is therefore our duty, as honest searchers after truth, to spare no efforts to eliminate from our thinking the prejudices which spring from our half-conscious wish for a favourable answer.

If we are to undertake any genuine consideration of the question of immortality the first essential is that we should have faced *the fact* of death fully, frankly, and with our whole being. The natural tendency is to ignore it in practice and sentimentalize it in theory. The Biblical story of the Fall, with subtle insight, starts its account of the history of the human struggle by emphasizing this. 'Ye shall not surely die,' said the serpent to Eve, 'ye shall be as gods, knowing good and evil.' So she and her partner ate of the fruit and achieved the knowledge of value; and the first result was that they knew their nakedness and procceded to hide it, and so to hide themselves from one another. 'Ye shall not surely die.' That was the writer's diagnosis of the first lie, the basic self-deception from which flowed all the sufferings and evil of human life. And equally, the redemption of man in Christian doctrine is held to be rooted in the death of Christ, in His full and complete acceptance of death for Himself and for mankind through Himself. There is, therefore, a devil's doctrine of immortality to be reckoned with in the voice that speaks within us and says: 'Ye shall not surely die. Death is an illusion. It is not really death.' Until that lie is finally slain in our own hearts, until with all our being we accept death as a reality, we cannot hope to find eternal life, or even to bring an unbiassed mind to the consideration of its possibility. For until we have really accepted death as one of the divine ordinances for human life, any doctrine of the immortality of the soul can only be another self-deception, another expression of our desire, in the face of the knowledge of good and evil, to hide our own nakedness from one another and from God. We must start any honest enquiry with the full recognition of the truth that the writer of the third chapter of Genesis puts into the mouth of God: 'Ye shall surely die.'

On the other hand, this assertion itself may be equally an effort to escape from the realities of our human situation. The denial of the immortality of the soul, quite as much as its assertion, may itself be subjective and may disguise an effort to ignore the realities of life. 'Let us eat and drink, for to-morrow we die' seems at first sight to involve the acceptance of our mortality. In fact, it does nothing of the sort. In that sense, all of us, whether we believe in immortality or deny it, accept the fact of death. But while one man may seek to escape from the fact by denying it—the attitude this which says 'Ye shall not *surely* die'—another may attempt to forget it by concentrating his attention upon, and engrossing his mind with, the momentary business of living. In both cases there is an intellectual assent to the fact of death, and a practical refusal of it. Both are acting as if the fact of death could be ignored in the business of living, as if it were not an integral part of life itself, and therefore could be discounted. Both attitudes involve pretence and self-deception.

For the *reality* of death is bound up, as the account of the Fall in Genesis insists, with the knowledge of good and evil. The assumption underlying both attitudes can be expressed in the hypothetical proposition: 'If death is real, life is meaningless.' But while one attitude denies the consequent, the other affirms the antecedent. The first says: 'Life is not meaningless, therefore death is not real.' The second says: 'Death is real, therefore life is meaningless.' The practical conclusions are different. The first goes on to assert that since death is unreal we can go on living by values which take no account of death. The second, having denied the significance of life, asserts that the only thing to be done is to live in a way that ignores values. The first is seeking to live by unreal values, since values which involve the ignoring of death must be unreal. The other seeks to live by the denial of all values, and, since that is impossible, it also is committed to unreality. The knowledge of good and evil can no more be escaped than the reality of death.

I have insisted on this point, by way of introduction, because it defines the personal approach to the question of immortality through which alone it can be made a real question or have any relevance to the realities of life. We must accept death first and completely; *then* we may go on to consider, with unbiassed minds, the question of immortality.

There has been in recent times a growing disbelief in the immortality of the soul. The main reason for that, so far as I can see, is one which is completely irrelevant. It is simply the shift of interest to the pressing problems of the world around us. Through the advance of scientific knowledge we find ourselves able, for the first time in history, to believe in the possibility of creating, in this world, the conditions of a satisfactory temporal existence. Whether we are right or not is neither here nor there. The point is that for the first time it is possible really to think so and to act on the thought. This means that one of the strongest motives for turning our attention to the possibility of a life hereafter which should compensate for the deficiencies of this life is removed. We are more inclined to concentrate on the immediate problems of temporal existence. But though this will explain to a large extent the disappearance of an effective belief in immortality, it has obviously no bearing upon the truth or falsity of that belief.

On the other hand, the development of science, particularly of physical science, has created an attitude of mind which makes it increasingly difficult to conceive a personal immortality. The main consideration which I wish to offer in this lecture is my conclusion that the so-called scientific evidence against the belief in immortality, though it necessarily makes havoc of certain traditional forms of the belief, is yet irrelevant to the main issue. This, of course, does nothing to establish the truth of immortality. It merely shows that most of the grounds on which immortality is denied rest upon a fundamental misconception.

We are so accustomed to think that science *is* knowledge that we overlook the fact that it *presupposes* knowledge. We have an immediate living experience of the world which is both more primitive and more concrete than any knowledge which is the result of deliberate reflection. Upon this all scientific knowledge is based. And this knowledge science can never deny without cutting the ground from under its feet. That life-knowledge not merely furnishes the basis upon which all science depends, but it differs in important respects from all other knowledge. In particular it has a completeness and reality about it which can never be achieved by reflection. For reflection forces us to disrupt the unity of life, to select one or another aspect of it, and put the others aside. The basic knowledge which is the soil in which all the achievements of science are rooted depends for its compulsive force upon the full relation between ourselves and the world. Primitively, we know things as we know persons, by loving or hating them, by living with them, by using them, by co-operating with them in practical life. And this knowledge is, in the last resort, the criterion by which all scientific theories are judged, as it is the reality to which they refer.

It is not merely in a general way that this living knowledge of things is presupposed in all scientific investigation, but also in particular detail. All the presuppositions which underlie science are derived from and verified in it. One of these, in particular, I should like you to notice. Science assumes the right to generalize from the observation of particular instances, to assert that what it finds in the individual reveals the nature of the universal. For this assumption there is no abstract logical basis. It arises from, and finds its justification in, that knowledge of the world which we have in the immediate experience of living. The thought of generalizing could never arise were it not for the fact that in our living we are immediately aware of the infinite in the finite. The infinite, which reflection can only represent as lying at the end of an interminable series, as being other than anything we can comprehend or express, is directly experienced everywhere and always in our unreflective activities. The effort of science to reach beyond the particularity of things to the universal laws which they express, is only an effort to reproduce in reflection the infinite which is known, face to face, in immediate experience.

On the other hand, science is only one form, and a limited form, of reflective knowledge. It seeks to understand things, in so far as they are material, that is to say, in so far as they can be measured and submitted to mathematical analysis. You will notice that I do not say that science is interested only in material things. For all things that we know are material, and nothing that we know in our immediate and concrete experience is merely material. Science is interested in everything in its material aspect, in everything so far as it is material, that is to say so far as it is stuff, so far as it can be manipulated and utilized. Beyond that its investigations do not, and cannot, go.

Now, if we take these two points together, we shall see that the infinite appears in scientific knowledge only in so far as it is material. That aspect of the infinite, as we are aware of it in life, is infinite Space-Time, and it is represented in reflective thought by the concepts of matter and energy, so that it comes about that the only *scientific* conception of the infinite is the idea of it as the complex of matter and energy, of which all individuals, so far as they are material, are particular expressions. In accordance with this conception of the infinite, the postulate of scientific investigation must be the doctrine of the conservation of matter and energy.

I have tried to indicate that the justification of scientific belief in the conservation of matter is only to be found in our immediate awareness of the infinite in the finite, so far as it is material. But that primary knowledge of the infinite is not confined to the material aspect of the world. In our immediate knowledge both of finite life and of finite personality we are aware of the infinite in other aspects. The tap-root of all scientific objection to a doctrine of personal immortality lies in the limitation of the infinite to its material aspect; or, at least, in the belief that the conservation of matter is the essential basis of such conservation as we experience above the material level. I want now to attempt to indicate that this limitation rests upon a misunderstanding.

All materialism which has any scientific basis implies the indestructibility of the elementary particles of which matter consists. How these elementary particles are described in current theory is irrelevant. The unit-realities of the material aspect of the world must be, on any scientific theory, imperishable. But what we call a *thing*, so far as it is material, is not imperishable, and its destruction is the disruption of the structure which holds together, in a spatio-temporal order, the unit particles of which it consists. There is, therefore, a sense in which everything material is imperishable. The matter of which it consists, and which is its only reality, so far as it is merely material, is immortal. So much the scientific materialist will admit. But he will go on to point out that the death of a living creature involves its dissolution into the material elements of which its body is composed, and that, though these elements are eternally conserved, the creature itself, as a temporary complex of these indestructible elements, cannot persist when the complex is disintegrated. Now this is undoubtedly true. But beyond and above this there remains something which is unexplained. I refer to the conservation of life in actual experience. Life is maintained from generation to generation through the processes of reproduction. And these are an essential feature of organic life. Certainly there is no ground for believing that a plant or animal is conserved as an individual beyond the time of its death. But life itself is conserved in the reproduction of new individuals from the old, and, whatever this conservation of life may be, it is certainly not the conservation of the material particles of which the individual's body is composed. There is, therefore, in the universe a conservation of life which is quite distinct from the conservation of matter.

The only point to which I would invite your attention in this connexion is that, within the limits of the life of an individual organism, the conservation of life does not depend upon the persistent identity of its material elements. On its material side life is a process of metabolism, in which the material elements of the body are being continually changed. It is probable that after a lapse of some years the unit-particles which originally composed the body of an organism have been entirely replaced by others. Yet the life of the organism has been conserved throughout the process. The dissolution of the material complex, so far from being identical with the death of the organism, is an essential element in its life. Thus, though it is true that the individual organism is not conserved beyond the point of death, it is also true that its death does not consist in the dissolution of the material complex which is its body. That dissolution is the *result* of the cessation of life. And the cessation of life is the cessation of the processes by which the continual dissolution of the body is continually overcome. The conservation of life, as we know it in experience, consists in the temporal continuity of functional processes which maintain and develop a form, independently of the identity of the matter in which that form is exhibited.

If we now turn to our experience, not of life, but of personality, we find again that it involves an immediate awareness of the infinite in the finite. Just as we experience infinite space in our experience of finite material objects, or the infinity of life in our experience of finite organisms, so we experience infinite personality in and through our experience of finite persons. And as a result of this there arises in reflection the problem of the conservation of personality. The immediate fact which confronts us in experience is the fact that personality is conserved throughout the life of any finite person. The question of personal immortality is directly related to the experience of the actual conservation of personality throughout the organic process of life. The ordinary way of raising the question is to ask: 'Does personality survive bodily death?' This question, largely because of its associations, is apt to be misleading. And I should like to raise the problem in another form. 'Does the conservation of personality, as we experience it in personal life, consist in or depend upon the conservation of the life of the organism?' If there is reason to conclude that it does not, then the question of the immortality of the soul will remain an open question. It will not be solved. But it will be released from all entanglement with questions about the conservation of organic life. In other words, the fact of bodily death will have been shown to be irrelevant to the question of personal immortality, just as we have seen how the fact of the conservation of matter is irrelevant to the question of the conservation of life.

The conservation of anything is a matter of its relation to time, and, therefore, the question 'How is personality conserved?' rests upon another question: 'How is personality related to time?' If we revert to the question of the conservation of matter, we can see that matter is conserved because the individual particles of which it consists are independent of time. They do not change. Matter, therefore, is subtemporal. This is to say that, from the standpoint of the real units of matter, time does not exist. They are the same, identical with themselves and unchanged, at all times. But this is not true of life. Life is essentially a temporal process depending upon a functional continuity in time. Any break in the temporal continuity in the life processes means the death of the organism. On the other hand, the conservation of life in the individual is not the persistence of a changeless self-identity. Life itself is a process of change or growth, and the infinity of life is that eternity of growth from generation to generation which we call evolution. The relation of organic life to time is, therefore, the most intimate relation possible. Time is of the essence of life. And life is essentially temporal. It is for this reason that the eternity of life can only be achieved through the continual reproduction of new individuals and new species. To say that life is essentially temporal is to say that organisms are essentially mortal, and that death is an essential element of organic life.

What we have now to ask is whether the relation of personality to time is of the organic type. If it is, there can be no personal immortality. If it is not, there may be. We can put this question in another form. 'Does the conservation of personality as we know it in finite experience depend *essentially* upon the continuity of temporal processes?' To that question I cannot profess to offer any conclusive answer here. But I should like to remind you of certain features of personal experience which suggest that it does not. In doing this I shall resist the temptation to refer to any but strictly normal experience. The field of abnormal experience is full of suggestive material, but I think that so far as research has yet gone such material is rightly suspect. I shall refer first to the familiar experience of sleep and unconsciousness. In sleep the normal processes of organic life go on. If they did not, we should die. But personality is in abeyance. Yet as soon as we recover consciousness we are immediately aware that personality has been conserved across the time-gap. To this extent, then, the conservation of personality is independent of temporal continuity. Personality does not fail to be conserved when there are time-gaps in personal consciousness.

In the second place, personality is bound up with the nature of rational consciousness. And this involves the capacity, as Plato put it, 'to look before and after'. This ability to transcend in consciousness the experience of the immediate present is a capacity, in some sense, to hold past or future existence within the limits of the temporal present, and involves a relation of the self to time which is completely different from the relation to time of either matter or organic life. For matter there is no past nor future. For life there is only a continuous advance from the present into the future. But for personality there is a freedom, in time, from time, which enables it, at least within limits, to be 'spectator of all time and all existence'. The limits of our personal consciousness extend far beyond the temporal limits of our organic life.

This obvious fact is not, as it is often represented, merely a feature of reflective thought. It is experienced in practical activity. When I determine an action through a memory of something that happened in my earlier experience, or through a knowledge of something that happened before I was born, there is an immediate relation between a past event and a present event. This relation is not mediated through a temporal continuity such as either mechanical or organic causality demands. It is as if in personality there lay the capacity to annihilate the time-gap separating the past from the present and to make the past, in its real pastness, an immediate determinant of the present. Here again, there is evidence that personality does not essentially depend, even in the practical sphere, upon the continuity of temporal processes.

We are familiar with experiences which we describe as living in the past or living in the future. If we consider what we mean when we use such phrases we shall find that they imply that the centre of personal life is not necessarily the temporal present. Action, so far as it is organic, must, of course, be action in the present. But a person's actions in the present, when considered not as events but as expressions of personality, may be focused and unified in an experience which is past. We know very well that the whole life of many a person is only explicable by the fact that his personality has its centre in early experience, and there are also many persons whose personal lives centre in the future and are explicable only in terms of expectation.

All these facts and many others like them indicate that the relation of personality to time is of a peculiar type, and in particular that the personal is not essentially temporal in the way that organic life certainly is. The conservation of personality, they suggest, is independent of, and not determined by, the continuity of temporal process which is the essence of the conservation of life. They suggest that personality is super-temporal, and that, in some sense, it includes time and yet is free of the limitations which belong to what is organic, so far as it is organic. I should go further and say that they show clearly that any argument against personal immortality which involves treating personality on the analogy of organic life must involve a misconception. Since the conservation of personality is of a different order from the conservation of life, it follows that the fact of death, indeed, the fact of the necessary mortality of the organic, does not in itself imply the mortality of the person.

That is as far as I can carry the argument at present. It does not at all prove any doctrine of personal immortality, but it does clear the ground and leave the field open. It also directs attention to the proper quarter. It is upon our experience of the conservation of personality, and upon the peculiar characteristics of the relation of personal experience to time and to temporal processes, that any discussion of the problem of immortality must be based. It is there that the data for drawing a conclusion are to be found, and that field has up to the present remained largely unexplored. But there is one theory of immortality which is definitely ruled out, the theory which I called to start with the Devil's doctrine of immortality. It is the conception of immortality as the persistence of the *organic* life beyond the point of death. Whatever is organic is mortal. And the death of the organism is the end of the organic life. But it is not necessarily the end of individual personality, nor even of personal consciousness. For personality is not inherently in time.

INDEX

INDEX

impulse, and will, 123
individual, and society, 95, 119
— and sex, 135
— and reality, 155
— and religion, 241
— conservation of the, 271, 278
individualism, is negation of religion, 65
— and intellect, 118
— involves isolation of selves, 229
individuality, personal, 157, 163
information, 147, 150ff.
initiative, 118
inspiration, 46
integrity, 135, 137
intellect, and action, 45
— education of, 76
— and individualism, 118
— and good conduct, 125
— and rationality, 201
intelligence, intellectual, 72
intuition, 156
irrationality, 205

Jesus, 40, 133f., 159, 171ff., 184, 210, 229, 241f., 247, 255, 263

Kant, 124, 208
knowledge, objective, 21, 55
— intellectual, 43

knowledge, emotional, 43
— a means to life, 86
— is always personal, 150
— is the grasp of reality, 155, 188

Language, 145, 191
Lawrence, D. H., 177
life, is activity, 23, 87
— organic and personal, 32, 93-115, 223f.
— emotional, 34ff., 77
— is awareness, 42, 235
— joy in living is end of, 90
— social, 179
— level, 219, 221
— and death, 264
— conservation of, 271f.
love, positive emotion, 31
— and sense-life, 42
— God is, 63, 223
— between two persons, 231
— and woman, 119
— and marriage, 126, 255
— sexual, 127, 135f., 140f.
— and interest, 188

Male and female, 134
Man, union of God and, 64
— and individuality and intellect, 119
— and woman, 133, 136, 255
— and communion, 250

282

INDEX

INDEX

Theology, 172, 192, 215
theory, and practice, 87
thinking, is not living, 74
thought, subsidiary to activity, 24
— and feeling, 25
— freedom of, 69
time, and personality, 275, 277f.
Trade Union, 99
tradition, 69, 94
— Roman, 124
truth, discovery of, 22, 262
— honesty of mind, 128ff.
— is one and indivisible, 181
— and rationality, 204

Unity, and woman, 119
— in friendship, 140, 149
— of family, 255
university of religion, 260

Utilitarianism, 47

Value, 31, 36
— judgment of, 37
— of science, 155
— and religion, 188
— of art, 155
— of life, 260, 265
virtue, 124

War, and science, 175
Whitehead, Professor, and religion, 225
will, free, 20
— and morality, 123
worship and religion, 183
woman, 100
— and emotion, 119
— and individualism, 120
— and social functions of sexes, 133
— and marriage, 255